The
Boca Raton
RESORT & CLUB

The Boca Raton
RESORT & CLUB
MIZNER'S INN

DONALD CURL
AND THE
BOCA RATON HISTORICAL SOCIETY

Charleston   London

THE
History
PRESS

Published by The History Press
Charleston, SC 29403
www.historypress.net

Cover photo by Peter Lorber.

First published 2008
Second printing 2010
Third printing 2011
Fourth printing 2011

Manufactured in the United States

ISBN 978.1.59629.527.8

Library of Congress Cataloging-in-Publication Data

Curl, Donald Walter, 1935-
The Boca Raton Resort and Club : Mizner's inn / Donald Curl and the Boca Raton Historical Society.
p. cm.
Includes bibliographical references.
ISBN 978-1-59629-527-8
1. Boca Raton Resort and Club--History. 2. Mizner, Addison, 1872-1933. 3. Hotels--Florida--Boca
Raton--History. 4. Resorts--Florida--Boca Raton--History. 5. Architecture--Florida--Boca Raton--
History. 6. Boca Raton (Fla.)--History. 7. Boca Raton (Fla.)--Biography. 8. Resort development--Florida-
-Boca Raton--History. 9. Boca Raton (Fla.)--Economic conditions. I. Boca Raton Historical Society. II.
Title.
TX941.B63C87 2008
917.59'3206--dc22
2008033430

Contents

Acknowledgements

Attempting to write any history demands the help of many people and organizations. A history of the Boca Raton Resort & Club obviously called upon many people from that organization. Russ Flicker, Anne Hersley-Hankins and Carole Boucard have been extremely kind to the Boca Raton Historical Society, as have so many others. I am particularly grateful to Morgan Green, who supplied access to recent photographs of the resort.

I also thank Peter and Addie Lorber and Courtenay Gilbert of Custom Photo Images. Peter is a nationally known, award-winning panorama photographer whose base of operations just happens to be Boca Raton, Florida. Over the years that I have researched the resort, Debi Murray and Tony Marconi of the Historical Society of Palm Beach County have always been extremely helpful, often in the most trying of circumstances. The same is true for Peg McCall, the Boca Raton Historical Society's former archivist. Mary Csar, the society's executive director, and Bonnie Dearborn, of the Florida Department of State's Division of Historical Resources, were always there to share their knowledge and their enthusiasm for the resort's history and its historic architecture. Fred Eckel read the entire manuscript and made many suggestions.

Finally, this work would never have happened without Susan Gillis, the Boca Raton Historical Society's curator of collections. Sue convinced me to undertake the writing, negotiated the contract, gathered the photographs, wrote the captions and constantly researched questions as they arose. Her artistic skills accomplished the layout and her technical skills put it all together and sent it to the publisher. Truly, she is my coauthor, though as they say, I am still responsible for all the errors.

Introduction

Two questions almost always arise when discussing Boca Raton: how do you pronounce it, and what does it mean? Solving the pronunciation riddle is easy. No one has a problem with Boca, though Raton has created arguments between those "in the know" and outsiders. The outsiders say "Rat-on," while residents use the long Spanish *o* and say "Ra-tone." Sometime before the 1920s, local residents tried to solve the problem for speakers of English by returning to the original "Ratone" spelling. When Addison Mizner came to town, he feared that this would create a problem for speakers of Spanish, and he once more dropped the final *e*. The real problem comes in translating its meaning from Spanish. Again, Boca is easy: it's a "mouth" or "opening," as in an inlet to the sea. Raton is difficult, and the most common translation is "rat." In the 1920s, Addison Mizner's publicity people said the name came from the rat-like shape of Lake Boca Raton. They also spun romantic tales of the pirates who used the lake to prey on coastal shipping and to hide from the Spanish and English navies. Obviously, those pirates also buried their treasure along the shores of the lake. Although over the years many have looked for these treasures, only a road-building crew in the 1920s actually found a few gold pieces, and legend claims that Wilson Mizner buried these pieces to spur land sales.

The problem is that "rat" in Spanish is *rata*, and *raton* means "mouse." Certainly, "Mouse's Mouth" is a preferable alternative to "Rat's Mouth," though many believe that neither is the true meaning of Boca Raton. *Raton* has been used as a nautical term in Spanish, meaning "hidden rocks that fret or wear away cables." So the correct translation could mean an inlet with hidden rocks. Did Boca Raton's inlet have "hidden rocks" that created navigational problems back in the 1500s? Unfortunately, the answer is probably no. What we know as Boca Raton inlet today was labeled on Spanish maps as late as the early nineteenth century as *Rio Seco*, or "Dry River," suggesting that no inlet existed.

Daniel Austin and David McJunkin attempt to reconcile the history of the name in their *Spanish River Papers* article titled "The Legends of Boca Raton." They point out that, between the late sixteenth century and the 1820s, Spanish and English maps showed Boca Raton (or *Ratones*) as an inlet on Northern Biscayne Bay in today's Miami-Dade County. Some maps even show a Ratone River flowing into Biscayne Bay. Only in the 1820s do maps show a Boca Ratones in its current location in southern Palm Beach County. Unfortunately, Austin and McJunkin conclude that the wonderful stories of pirates and hidden gold are borrowed, along with the name, from Miami-Dade County.

Austin and McJunkin also weigh in on the translation problem by suggesting a third translation for *raton*. They point out that some scholars trace the origin of the word to *ladron cobarde* or "cowardly thief," making Boca Raton a thieves' inlet. They document settlements of outlaws hiding from Spanish authorities on Biscayne Bay as early as the sixteenth century. They also tell of a Spanish monk, left by Pedro Menéndez de Avilés to establish a mission at a Tequesta Indian village on upper Biscayne Bay. They say his reports, like those of missionaries to the same village two centuries later, complain that the Indians were thieves—a good reason for naming the site Boca Raton, or "Thieves' Inlet." Today, translations really have no importance. For most who see the name, Boca Raton means one of Florida's most outstanding communities; a quality place to live, work and play.

Chapter 1

Mizner's Inn

Addison Mizner is the most widely known name in Boca Raton, where you might live in an apartment in Mizner Tower, purchased through Addison Mizner Realty with financing from Addison Mizner Mortgage Company; send your children to Addison Mizner School; shop at Mizner Park; visit friends at the oceanfront Addison condominium or in Mizner Forest; take your dog for a run at Mizner Bark; or eat dinner at the Addison Restaurant. On your way to the various "Mizner" destinations, you might pass his statue in Royal Palm Place on the corner of Mizner Boulevard and South Federal Highway. Although Addison Mizner spent no more than a year of his life in Boca Raton, and never really lived in the city, his design for the small inn on Lake Boca Raton and his dream for the new resort city have indelibly linked the Mizner name and Boca Raton.

Who was Addison Cairns Mizner? Although there have been four serious studies written about the man and his architecture, and he published the first volume of his autobiography and was completing the second when he died, what most people remember are the myths and half-truths found in a book written by Alva Johnson: that he was an "untrained" architect who was unable to "draw" blueprints, that he sketched plans for clients in the sand at the beach and that he frequently left out stairs, bathrooms and other necessities when planning his houses. Alice De Lamar, a close friend of the architect and the person responsible for the magnificent tribute to him, *Florida Architecture of Addison Mizner*, later claimed that Johnson did his Mizner research in Palm Beach bars. Perhaps we prefer bar stories to the truth. In reality, Mizner was broadly trained as an architect, could draft plans and had a real talent for sketching out his ideas. He also always had excellent architects and draftsmen in his office to tell him if he forgot a staircase.

Addison Mizner was born in Benicia, California, in 1872, the seventh of eight children of Lansing Bond and Ella Watson Mizner. His father, an attorney and politician, actively campaigned for the election of Benjamin Harrison for the presidency in 1888. As his reward, President Harrison appointed him minister to Central America, which included the five republics of Guatemala, Honduras, El Salvador, Nicaragua and Costa Rica. The

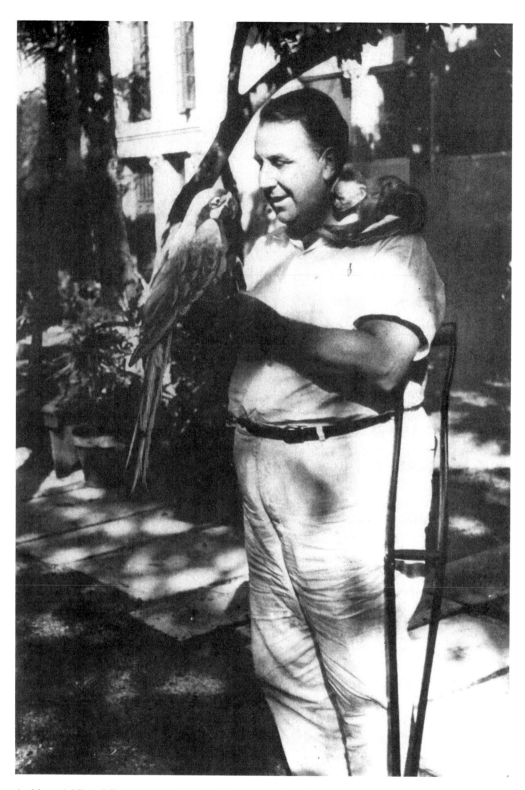

Architect Addison Mizner poses with his pet bird and monkey (Johnny Brown) in Palm Beach in the 1920s. *Photo courtesy Donald W. Curl.*

sixteen-year-old Addison had injured his ankle jumping over a bonfire the previous July Fourth, and his parents decided to take him and his younger brother Wilson with them to Guatemala City.

Although Addison spent only a year in Central America, it became a defining period in his life. He learned the Spanish language, and while traveling throughout the five republics with his father, he developed an appreciation for Spanish Colonial art and architecture. When his informal and checkered secondary education failed to earn him admission to the University of California, his abilities in the Spanish language and his love of Spanish culture prompted him to study at the University of Salamanca in Spain. Although never formally enrolled in a degree program, his year at the university gave him a profound appreciation for the unique beauty of Spanish architecture as it had developed through the centuries and allowed him to begin his study by sketching its great examples.

After extensive travel in Europe and the Far East, Mizner decided to become an architect and joined the San Francisco office of Willis Polk as an apprentice. Polk, a young man only five years Mizner's senior, had himself apprenticed in St. Louis. Polk became a much-honored architect, although in 1893 he had just opened his own office and, as Mizner said, was a "young architect of great taste and little work." In his three years as Polk's apprentice, Mizner became actively involved in the entire design process. He spent long hours at the drafting board and reading from Polk's impressive architectural library. Also under Polk's direction, Mizner learned the fundamentals of the building trades. He gave his mentor credit for his abilities as a plumber, carpenter, electrician, bricklayer and plasterer. Mizner became a well-trained architect, as did many of his colleagues at the time, through the apprentice system. Moreover, his self-study and travel experiences combined to give him impressive credentials for his chosen profession.

After a series of adventures in Alaska during the gold rush, in Hawaii and again in the Far East, in 1905 Mizner opened an architecture office and began a country house practice in New York City. Through childhood friends from San Francisco, Mrs. Hermann Oelrichs and her sister, Mrs. William K. Vanderbilt Jr., the young architect received the introductions and made the social contacts necessary to build his practice. Of the sixteen known commissions he completed in the next eleven years, one Long Island country house later became the home of Marjorie Merriweather Post and today houses offices for the Post Campus of Long Island University.

America's entry into World War I in 1917 meant the end to almost all private building. Moreover, Mizner had reinjured his ankle. Paris Singer, an heir to the sewing machine fortune and a New York friend, invited the ailing Mizner to Palm Beach for the 1918 season. There, Paris commissioned the architect to design a convalescents' hospital for shell-shocked soldiers that could later become a private club. The war ended before Mizner completed the hospital, and Singer opened his new building in January 1919 as the exclusive Everglades Club.

In 1919, Palm Beach resort society centered on the hotels built by Henry M. Flagler as he extended his coastal railroad south from Jacksonville. The lakefront Royal Poinciana Hotel opened in February 1894 with 540 rooms. It proved so popular, attracting America's financial and social elite, that he built a second hotel on the oceanfront in 1896 called the

Palm Beach Inn. This, too, proved successful, and after several additions, in 1900 he changed its name to The Breakers. The Royal Poinciana also underwent additions, so by 1901 it contained 1,081 rooms and could advertise itself as the largest wooden resort in the world. Until the founding of the Everglades Club, a typical resort day included breakfast in the hotel dining rooms, mornings on The Breakers' beach, lunch at the hotels, afternoon sightseeing—or golf and tennis for the sports minded—a tea dance at the Royal Poinciana's Cocoanut Grove and then a formal hotel dinner. Most hotel guests changed clothes for each of these activities. Their costumes ranged from "modest" bathing suits to long gowns and important jewels for women and black tie for men at dinner.

With the exception of Colonel Edward R. Bradley's Beach Club, the resort's gambling casino, visitors to Palm Beach had no alternative to the hotels' entertainment. They even determined the resort's season. The hotels opened in early January and closed shortly after the Washington Birthday Ball held on February 22 at the Royal Poinciana. The short season also meant that very few visitors had built houses in Palm Beach. The Everglades Club prompted both a social and architectural revolution in the resort.

As a new and exclusive resort venue, the club helped promote the trend toward greater informality than was permitted in the hotels. Singer led the way by introducing Riviera-style day wear, though evenings remained strictly formal. Singer chose the resort's three hundred wealthiest and most socially prominent citizens as club members. These members almost completely abandoned the old hotels, and many now decided to build vacation villas in the town. These decisions resulted in the lengthening of the social season and the acceptance of Mizner's architecture as the new standard for Palm Beach. His architecture, an eclectic blend of Spanish, Italian, Moorish and Venetian motifs from many periods, created a romantic and playful alternative to the drab wooden architecture of the Flagler hotel period. Mizner's lofty towers overlooking rambling hand-made tile roofs; rough stucco walls with columns, doors and window surrounds of cast stone; his restrained decorative details; and his open floor plans introduced a new form of Mediterranean architecture to Florida. He understood that the climate had made Palm Beach America's leading winter resort. His houses, clubs and even commercial structures used many windows and doors to both bring the outdoors in and provide quick access to the outside. Broad terraces overlooking the ocean or Lake Worth and private patios and secluded courts all seemed completely at home in a tropical setting and became the trademarks of his buildings.

Eva Stotesbury, the wife of banker and J.P. Morgan partner Edward Stotesbury and *grand dame* of Palm Beach society, confirmed the architect's status in the community when she fired her Philadelphia architect and hired Mizner to design El Mirasol ("the Sunflower"), her planned oceanfront mansion. Within the next five years, Mizner completed nearly fifty commissions in the town. These included vacation villas for America's social and business leaders such as the Munn brothers, John S. Phipps, Barclay Warburton, Anthony J. Drexel Biddle, Joseph Cosden, Angier Duke, Edward Shearson, Rodman Wanamaker, William Gray Warden and Harold Vanderbilt. Moreover, the other architects of his day, Marion Sims Wyeth, Maurice Fatio and John Volk, all designed in the same Mediterranean style. By the mid-1920s, Palm Beach could have passed as a historic village on the Mediterranean seashore.

By 1925, all of Florida, and particularly the southeastern coast, had become involved in a great real estate boom. Beginning in the 1890s, Flagler's Florida East Coast Railway had first introduced tourists to America's tropical paradise. In the early days, only the well-to-do who could afford long winter vacations made the trip. After World War I, the Dixie Highway connected Florida to the populous cities of the Northeast and Midwest. The mass production of inexpensive automobiles allowed the growing American middle class to come to the state. While the winter climate remained the one constant that drew visitors, the growing prosperity of the Coolidge years greatly increased their numbers. The Coolidge prosperity also convinced many that everyone could be rich. The stories of early investors in Florida land helped fuel the boom, as did Florida's promise never to impose state income or inheritance taxes. By the 1920s, many Americans sought an alternative to life in the increasingly industrialized, crowded and dirty Northern cities. Florida remained the last American frontier. As one commentator said, the state offered the best of two worlds: "Latin excitement and American plumbing."

The great Florida developments, like Carl Fisher's Miami Beach, George Merrick's Coral Gables and Joseph Young's Hollywood, also helped to encourage the boom. These and dozens of other smaller subdivisions promoted both the quality of Florida life and the profits to be made through investing in Florida real estate. They all spent lavishly on advertising. Fisher's wintertime New York City billboard picturing his attractive, bathing-suit-clad wife on the beach with the caption "Its June in Miami Beach" set the standard. While recognizing the importance of advertising, the developers also realized they needed to provide the amenities of Florida life. With Americans' growing interest in sports, almost all promised golf courses, tennis courts, swimming pools and bathing beaches. The more ambitious also added polo fields. The major promotions all had a hotel as a basic attraction—a place where the prospective landowner could stay while selecting and purchasing his lots.

Mizner had watched the real estate frenzy build. By 1924, the excitement generated by the boom and the prospect of great wealth proved too much for him. As a Palm Beach society architect, he numbered among his clients some of the nation's wealthiest citizens. While his practice had provided a good life, it produced no great wealth. When he decided to become a developer, he first purchased land at "Mizner Beach" in Boynton, which later became Ocean Ridge. His decision to move Ocean Boulevard away from the ocean to provide beachfront lots caused such great opposition from local citizens that Mizner scrapped the project.

In 1925, he directed his interest to the little farming town of Boca Raton, twenty-five miles south of Palm Beach. In March, the *Palm Beach Post* said that former Mizner client Rodman Wanamaker had purchased three-quarters of a mile of beachfront property in the town for $1 million. On April 15, Mizner announced that Wanamaker purchased the land for the Mizner Development Corporation. He also unveiled sketches for the one-thousand-room Castillo de Rey, "the world's most complete and artistic hostelry," and plans for the new development, "the world's most architecturally beautiful playground." These included immediate construction of Donald Ross–designed golf courses, a polo field, a casino and $1 million in other improvements such as canals, parks, plazas and paved and landscaped streets. The very size of the project made it one of the greatest of

Where is Boca Raton?

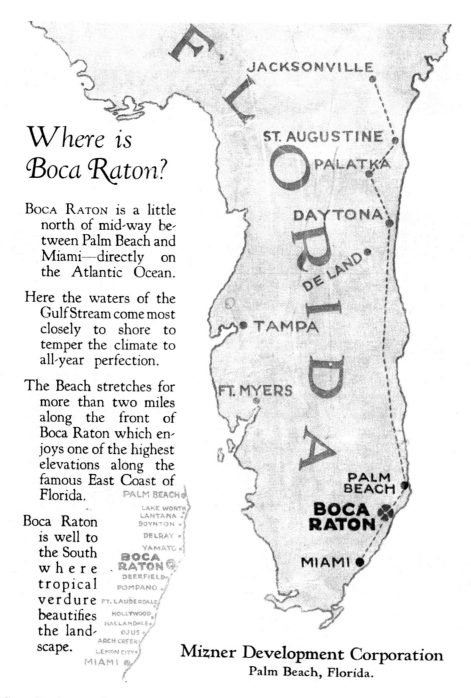

BOCA RATON is a little north of mid-way between Palm Beach and Miami—directly on the Atlantic Ocean.

Here the waters of the Gulf Stream come most closely to shore to temper the climate to all-year perfection.

The Beach stretches for more than two miles along the front of Boca Raton which enjoys one of the highest elevations along the famous East Coast of Florida.

Boca Raton is well to the South where tropical verdure beautifies the landscape.

Mizner Development Corporation
Palm Beach, Florida.

The Mizner Development Corporation put the small farming town of Boca Raton "on the map" in 1925 with the announcement of its "Boca Raton" development project. *Boca Raton Historical Society.*

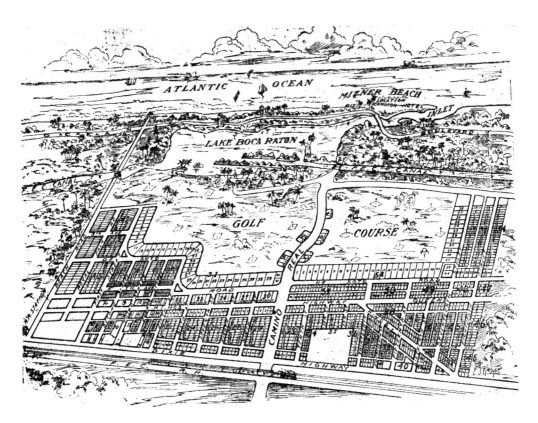

This map for Mizner's Boca Raton development shows the site of the Cloister Inn and golf courses on the west side of Lake Boca Raton, opposite the never-built Ritz-Carlton at "Mizner Beach." *Boca Raton Historical Society.*

Florida's boom-time developments. The possibilities of large profits certainly appealed to Mizner, though so did the ability to create an entire city, to supervise town planning, to veto unappealing buildings and to design the most important structures himself. Boca Raton excited the artist in the architect.

The board of the development corporation included well-known leaders of the nation's social, business and entertainment worlds. Many had been former Mizner clients and all had Palm Beach connections. T. Coleman du Pont—who, along with his two du Pont cousins, had established the modern E.I. du Pont de Nemours Company—served as chairman. Other board members included Harold Vanderbilt; Lytle Hull, a real estate investor; Paris Singer; Irving Berlin, the songwriter; Madame Frances Alda, the opera star; W.C. Robinson, a large New York building contractor; D.H. Conkling, publisher of the *Palm Beach Post*; Elizabeth Arden; Clarence H. Geist, the Philadelphia utilities magnate; and Rodman Wanamaker, the department store heir.

Under the direction of Harry Reichenbach, a professional press agent, the company launched a national advertisement campaign that prominently displayed the names of the board members. The full-page ads showed sketches of the oceanfront hotel, plat plans of the new resort, told how Mizner "the inspired architect" planned to make Boca Raton "the Dream City of the Western World" and, in general, combined the idea that

The Mizner Development Corporation publicity promised that the Boca Raton development would be the "greatest resort in the world" (a few years hence). *Boca Raton Historical Society.*

In 1925, Mizner revealed his plans for the one-thousand-room (Ritz-Carlton) Castillo del Rey, "the world's most complete and artistic hostelry," on the beach at Boca Raton. It was never constructed. *Boca Raton Historical Society*.

the town would become one of the world's most desirable places to live and an unrivaled investment opportunity: a mixture of "snob appeal and greed appeal." An advertisement in the *Palm Beach Post* in May stated:

> *The owners and controllers of the Mizner Development Corporation are a group of very rich men—men of unlimited means, who propose to build from the creative genius of Addison Mizner, what will probably be the most wonderful resort city in the world…the combined wealth of the stockholders…probably represents considerably over one-third of the entire wealth of the United States…It is reasonable to suppose that every lot buyer… should make quick and large profits.*

On May 16, the Mizner Development Corporation announced that its first group of lots had sold out for over $2 million on the first day. It also said that the Ritz-Carlton Investment Corporation planned to take over Mizner's oceanfront hotel. Since the Ritz-Carlton organization took pride in the quality of its service, it would reduce the size of the hotel to seven hundred rooms. While Mizner remained the architect of the hotel's exterior, the New York architectural firm of Warren & Wetmore, the designers of Grand Central Terminal and several Ritz-Carlton hotels, received the commission for the interior plans.

Although greatly pleased by the Ritz-Carlton action, Mizner knew that the Warren & Wetmore participation meant delaying the start of construction. Since, like other Florida developers, he believed he needed a hotel to promote land sales, on May 23 he proposed to build a small inn of only one hundred rooms on the west side of Lake Boca Raton. From the first, Mizner rushed construction of his small inn. As he completed the plans that included a lakefront cloister enclosing a large courtyard, he announced a January 1926 opening for the now-named Cloister Inn.

Throughout the summer, the Mizner organization continued to advertise projects designed to sell lots in its development. These included an airport, a deepened inlet and yacht basin, a Venetian lake with gondolas, a Spanish village and a cabaret owned and managed by Mizner friend and company board member Irving Berlin that "promised the best theatrical talent of America and Europe." Summer also saw the plans for Ritz-

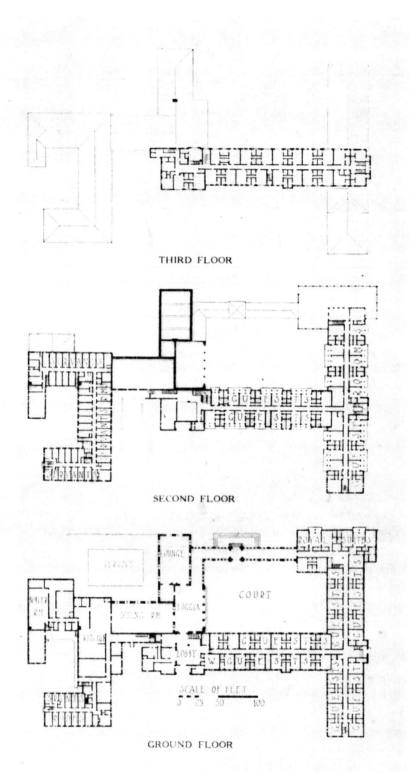

THIRD FLOOR

SECOND FLOOR

GROUND FLOOR

This plan reveals the three floors of Mizner's small Cloister Inn. Today, this comprises the southeastern corner of the Boca Raton Resort & Club. *Photo courtesy Donald W. Curl.*

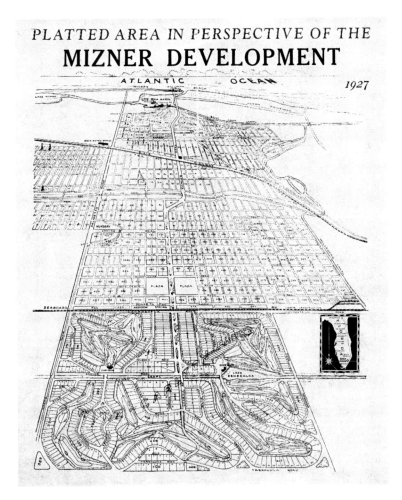

PLATTED AREA IN PERSPECTIVE OF THE
MIZNER DEVELOPMENT
1927

This map, looking east, shows the Mizner Development Corporation's plan for Boca Raton. The street at left is Palmetto Park Road; the rail line in the foreground is today's Amtrak route. *Boca Raton Historical Society.*

Carlton Park, a golf course community to the west of the city. To connect the park to the Ritz-Carlton Hotel, Mizner proposed the 160-foot-wide Camino Real. The road began at the beach, crossed the Intracoastal over a Mizner-designed Venetian bridge with a tower apartment for the bridge keeper, and continued westward, ending two and a half miles from the ocean in Ritz-Carlton Park. Camino Real's route passed the Administration Buildings, designed by Mizner to house his company's offices, and a series of projected shopping arcades similar to the architect's Via Mizner and Via Parigi in Palm Beach. Here, Mizner proposed a center canal modeled on the Botofago of Rio de Janeiro. From there, Camino Real passed through a large, open plaza with its proposed Addison Station at the Seaboard Railway tracks and his planned Episcopal church dedicated to his mother. As it continued westward, it widened to 220 feet, and Mizner planned a center canal with a series of attractive waterfalls. The flowing water, supplied by heavy rains, prevented mosquitoes from breeding in its waters.

Land sales remained high, climbing to $6 million by the summer. The Mizner organization opened offices in Palm Beach, Miami, Miami Beach and Tampa, and in many Northern cities. It also continued its lavish advertising campaign. One full-page

Mizner's plans for Boca Raton included his own home, a castle sited on a small island in Lake Boca Raton. It was also never completed. *Boca Raton Historical Society.*

broadside proclaimed that "Florida sands are the greatest gold mine ever discovered" and mentioned that a "deluxe Pullman bus leaves the Miami office for Boca Raton daily except Sunday at 10 a.m." In early September, Mizner released sketches of his own proposed home, a castle on a small man-made island in Lake Boca Raton. The architect said it harkened back to the days when "Goths swaggered down from the north, leaving on cities, walls, and fortress-like castles the marks of their genius for war, government, and architecture." As inspiration for the castle, he imagined a

> *Spanish fortress of the Twelfth Century captured from its owner by a stronger enemy, who, after taking it, adds on one wing and another—and then loses it in turn to another who builds to suit his taste...Perhaps later, the whole thing is restored to the Gothic period.*

The top floor of the tower contained a mirador, and other floors had guest rooms and the owner's own bedroom with a projecting balcony bathroom. The ground floor contained a great hall, a thirty-six- by fifty-two-foot drawing room, a dining room with Mizner's Salamanca linen-fold panels from his Villa Mizner apartment, a loggia and a kitchen and butler's pantry. In reality, the castle was a more elaborate version of the Villa Mizner. The lower level had a "boat grotto" to house a forty-five-foot yacht, a wine cellar and rooms for servants and caretakers. An elevator connected the floors and a drawbridge operated by electric motors protected the castle from intruders. H.B. Sayles, a former draftsman in Mizner's office who drew the plans for the castle, claimed it would have cost well over $1 million, "but Mr. M. didn't worry much about cost." Mizner promised to leave the castle to Boca Raton for a museum.

While Mizner continued to rush completion of the Cloister Inn and other improvements that he hoped might promote land sales, by the fall of 1925 these sales began to slow. The summer had shown signs that the land boom might be in trouble. During the 1920s, Florida, and particularly southeastern Florida, still remained oriented to the winter season. In the summer, most hotels and restaurants closed, as did stores and other facilities that mainly served tourists. Over the summer of 1925, thousands of Northerners decided to take their summer vacations in Florida. Loading their families in automobiles, they streamed down the Dixie Highway. As the numerous real estate salesmen and construction workers who migrated to Florida for the economic opportunities had already swollen the summer population and taxed its facilities, the summer tourists found their only shelter in hastily erected tent cities and their own cars. With few restaurants open and grocery stores having no fresh vegetables or milk, ice shortages because of the great demand, power outages common and even water supplies unreliable, the poor tourists still had to face South Florida's most prevalent summer problem of the era: clouds of hungry mosquitoes. The pleasant summer vacation to see what the boom was all about quickly became a nightmare. These tourists wasted no time in returning home and blasting Florida to everyone they met.

This aerial view looking west across Lake Boca Raton shows the Cloister Inn and adjacent golf courses nearing completion in late 1925. *Boca Raton Historical Society.*

In August 1925, the Florida East Coast Railway announced that freight car congestion in every South Florida city forced it to impose an embargo on all but perishable goods. The other railroads quickly followed suit. The high wages for construction workers produced a shortage of manual labor to unload the freight cars. The railroads claimed that while a hundred cars came into the area every day, only eighty were unloaded. Mizner and other developers depended upon outside supplies to continue their building programs. They depended upon their building programs to continue to sell lots in their developments.

Late summer also saw a campaign waged in Northern newspapers to warn investors about the fraudulent claims of Florida promoters. One Ohio newspaper called Florida "the paradise of get-rich-quick gentry." Other newspapers said that if "by-the-sea was part of the name, it probably was not," while another claimed that land sold in the winter was often covered by several feet of water during the rainy months of summer—the old Florida tale of land selling "by the gallon." Most warned that the speculation had greatly overpriced the true value of the land. At an early October conference organized by a number of Florida businessmen meeting at T. Coleman du Pont's Waldorf-Astoria Hotel in New York, Florida Governor John W. Martin declared the state a victim of misrepresentation and called upon its leaders to fight for the truth. Other speakers at this "Truth about Florida" conference called for "truth in the news which comes or purports to come from Florida." Most speakers emphasized that the real estate activity in Florida and its greatly enhanced land values represented real worth and not a boom. The *New York Times* remained unconvinced and said the conference proved that Florida businessmen had second thoughts about the boom.

As the questions about the health of the boom arose, many investors and potential investors began to feel uncomfortable about the Florida scene. Booms are based on confidence and optimism: what is bought today will be worth as much, if not more, tomorrow. When questions arise, many stop buying. Although the sales of property in Boca Raton began to slow, Mizner still rushed his inn to completion and announced other projects that he hoped gave people confidence in the development. Mizner also continued his full-page advertisements, particularly in the *Palm Beach Post*, whose publisher, D.H. Conkling, accepted additional company stock for their publication. By October, most ads stressed two concepts. First, that "they are building to live in Boca Raton" emphasized the many projects under construction in the town. Harry Vought and Company offered "Beautiful Homes at Boca Raton" for $7,000, ready for occupancy in early January 1926. The modest homes had thirteen- by twenty-one-foot living rooms with high-beamed pecky cypress ceilings, two bedrooms, a bath, a kitchen and a breakfast room, "giving ample accommodations for the average size family." Vought, the builder of the Mizner-designed Via Parigi on Worth Avenue, urged buyers to both "think of the joy of living in Boca Raton" and "the gratifying profit [on such] an investment." The Vought company had twenty-two houses under construction and planned to build a total of fifty. A company advertisement claimed that the man with a small winter cottage could say Addison Mizner, "who has built the most exclusive homes in Palm Beach, is also the architect of his home."

The second concept stressed by Mizner publicity was the guarantee that the company would complete all of the amenities detailed in its advertisements. These included the

Beautiful Homes at BOCA RATON $7,000

Ready for Occupancy Jan. 10TH

The first homes in Boca Raton!

Only five minutes from the CLOISTER!

These charming Spanish bungalows have a large living-room with high ceiling and beautiful finish in cypress; two large bedrooms with spacious closets, kitchen, breakfast-room and bath.

Every home has been approved for design and construction by Addison Mizner.

When completed, each home will be a gem of beauty on a landscaped plot, 45x100. These homes are in Plat 11 of the MIZNER Development —just west of the Dixie Highway, on fine, sloping ground.

Here, the home-life of Boca Raton will begin and the home-lover who will go to Boca Raton NOW and see The CLOISTER nearing completion —EL CAMINO REAL being paved—the site for the magnificent new RITZ-CARLTON being excavated—Lakes and Canals being dredged— golf courses being laid down—will recognize what a wonderful offering these homes are at $7,000.

Of course, so much for so little could be offered only in the pre-development period of BOCA RATON. And, only those with vision and fore-sight will take advantage of this offer, which we reserve the right to with-draw at our option.

Aside from the joy of living at BOCA RATON, think of the opportuni-ties for realizing a most gratifying profit on such an investment. It is around these homes that the great residential resort is being built. The price— $7,000—the terms—attractive.

Go down to Boca Raton today and inspect one of the sample houses. Ask for our own representative at the Administration building.

If more convenient, arrangements to visit Boca Raton may be made at the office of the Mizner Development Corporation. De Luxe Pull-men Bus leaves the Palm Beach office daily except Sunday at 9:30 A. M.

Harry Vought & Co., Inc.
·:· BUILDERS ·:·

OFFICE
Via Mizner
Palm Beach
Phone 1375

DIRECTORS
H. H. VOUGHT, JR., President
DOUGLAS VOUGHT
M. HALPERN, Vice-Pres. and Treas.

This Mizner Development Corporation ad for "Beautiful Homes at Boca Raton" featured modest homes by contractor Harry Vought. Today, this neighborhood is known as "Spanish Village." *Boca Raton Historical Society.*

BOCA RATON
Where Promises Are as Good as the God-Given Soil

And here are the promises of the MIZNER DEVELOPMENT CORPORATION:

A NEW, MAGNIFICENT RITZ-CARLTON HOTEL OF 700 ROOMS
THE NEW, SPLENDID CLOISTER OF 100 ROOMS
THE CAMINO REAL—160 FEET WIDE—BISECTING THE DEVELOPMENT
LAKE AND CANALS DREDGED   POLO FIELDS
THREE GOLF COURSES
AN ARTIFICIAL LAKE, ⅓ BY ⅜ OF A MILE IN SIZE
TENNIS COURTS

NO STREET will be less than sixty feet wide and many will be eighty feet wide. All streets will be paved for their full width and there will be private beaches restricted against all intrusion.

ADDISON MIZNER — the man who is planning the city —is building at BOCA RATON a house to cost one million dollars and will live there himself.

Every promise of the MIZNER DEVELOPMENT CORPORATION is made to be kept. Exaggeration has no place in BOCA RATON's lexicon. The very names of the men associated with the development are an assurance of faith and the guaranty above, coming

from these men, is merely throwing of a spotlight onto the Sun.

As FLORIDA grows — and it is expanding at a greater rate than has ever been noted before in the annals of migration — its fairest spot — its most endowed acreage

BOCA RATON

must grow—must thrive—at a faster rate than other less-favored spots.

A glance ahead will assure you as no argument can, that BOCA RATON is the magnet for the best — the most exacting — the most cynical element in the world. And—

AN INVESTMENT TODAY IN BOCA RATON SOIL IS AN ANTICIPATION OF POTENTIAL PROFIT—OF RESIDENTIAL SECURITY

READ this advertisement. Analyze the promises. Note the names of the men who make the guaranty. Then—ACT. Act while BOCA RATON is in the pre-development stage, for as sure as the new day comes —new VALUES come.

Mizner Development Corporation
Developers of BOCA RATON Florida

This Mizner Development Corporation advertisement sought to reassure investors of the legitimacy of the project amidst national concerns about the Florida land boom. *Boca Raton Historical Society.*

Ritz-Carlton Hotel, the Cloister Inn, the 160-foot-wide Camino Real, the dredged lakes and canals, a polo field, three golf courses and tennis courts. As one ad stated, "Boca Raton, where Promises Are as Good as the God-Given Soil." The company urged readers of the ad to "note the names who make this guaranty." To further reassure its potential customers, Boca Raton advertisements could be attached to deeds and "become a part thereof." A November editorial in Conkling's *Palm Beach Post* commended the company, saying that this gave confidence to the public that Florida's real estate had true value, as any company that made this promise "imposes upon itself a voluntary obligation to tell the truth." Conkling, of course, owned a great deal of stock in the Mizner company.

In late October, the company's board met in Palm Beach, and du Pont and several other members resigned. They objected to the use of their names in company advertisements, claiming that the ads made them personally responsible for guaranteeing Boca Raton's construction. They particularly objected to attaching the ads to deeds. Mizner publicity claimed the board members resigned over differences on board membership, implying that du Pont wished to elect friends to the board and had failed. Angered at this statement, the newly resigned board members said in a November letter to the *New York Times* that they had little financial interest in the Mizner company and they objected to the use of their names in advertisements. They left the board after company officers met their attempt "to eliminate exaggerated publicity" with "criticism rather than cooperation."

October 1925 marked the high point for all land sales in Florida. It was also the last month of large land sales in Boca Raton. Mizner's development was seen as one of the best. His architectural and artistic leadership, and du Pont's business abilities, seemed to ensure its success. Du Pont's resignation from the board signaled that even Boca Raton might be in trouble. One writer suggested the resignation "threw a wet blanket" over the entire boom. Certainly, Boca Raton real estate sales plummeted. Mizner, who needed sales to continue the construction of the Cloister Inn, the many other promised improvements and to make payments on the land he had purchased for the development, pushed on. The company began selling lots in the exclusive Distrito de Boca Raton, the city's most expensive subdivision, and opened a restaurant at the new Administration Buildings, where prospective real estate buyers could have al fresco lunch, tea and dinner on the patio.

Mizner designed both the Cloister Inn and the Administration Buildings to serve as prototypes of the architecture of the new city. As everyone who visited Boca Raton saw these buildings, Mizner lavished his time and talents on them. As inspiration for the north Administration Building, he chose El Greco's house and studio in Toledo, Spain—buildings he particularly admired. Its enclosed patio with its hanging galleries, small fountain and canvas awning supported from large wrought-iron rings echoed El Greco's house, as did the open porch on the southern façade. Even the "cannonball" capitals on the columns supporting the porch could be found on the Toledo building. The northern façade had a Spanish baroque door surround similar to the entrance to El Greco's studio. On the interior, Mizner modeled a small room on the El Greco kitchen, with masses of polychrome tiles. The southern building housed the drafting rooms on its second floor and a kitchen for the restaurant in its northwest wing. A small apartment on the second floor served as Mizner's retreat. The buildings both offered visitors an excellent example of Mizner's proposed Boca Raton.

To complete construction of the Cloister Inn and his other projects, Mizner was forced to borrow money. Even with these additional resources, he had to use the products of his various industries to save money. When construction started on the Everglades Club, he discovered that he needed to make his own roof tiles as the commercially produced American tiles failed to satisfy for authenticity. Singer established a pottery with three kilns to fire tiles for the club and had Mizner take over other businesses to produce wrought-iron lighting fixtures and ornamental grills, as well as make furniture for the new building. After the club opened, Singer allowed Mizner to purchase the kilns, and

The Administration Buildings, located at Dixie Highway and Camino Real, served as headquarters for Mizner's development. The northernmost building was inspired by El Greco's home in Toledo. *Boca Raton Historical Society.*

he established Las Manos Potteries, which made both his roof and floor tiles and, later, decorative pottery. This became the first of the Mizner Industries. As Singer sold the other businesses, Mizner began to reassemble these craft works as he received more and more commissions. These included blacksmith shops for his ornamental wrought-iron grills, gates, fire screens, andirons and other hardware; a cast-stone plant for his window and door surrounds, columns, capitals and balustrades; and a furniture factory to produce the "antique" reproductions he needed to properly furnish his buildings. At first his products served his own commissions, though soon other South Florida architects began to specify items from Mizner Industries, which quickly became West Palm Beach's largest employer.

A January 1926 *Palm Beach Post* article said that thirty craftsmen at the Mizner furniture factory had worked overtime for the last three months to furnish the new hotel. The furniture, "distinctive copies of antiques," for the guest rooms included "220 bed 'heads,' copied after notable examples of the Spanish" with "their illumined saints and crests and emblems"; 120 telephone stands; 100 dressing tables; 110 mirrors; 100 writing tables; and 110 three-drawer dressing tables. The article set the cost of the inn at $10,000 a room, or $1 million, "making it one of the best appointed and most

MIZNER INDUSTRIES INCORPORATED

MANUFACTURERS OF

POTTERY · ROOF & FLOOR TILE · PERIOD FURNITURE · WICKER · UPHOLSTERING · REPAIRING
ANTIQUE MILLWORK AND HARDWARE · BRONZE SASH · WROUGHT IRON
STAINED AND LEADED GLASS WINDOWS · RECONSTRUCTED AND
ORNAMENTAL STONE · IMITATION MARBLE

Factories:
PENN ROAD
WEST PALM BEACH
FLORIDA

337 Worth Avenue
P. O. Box 2068
PALM BEACH, FLORIDA

Telephones:
OFFICE 2-1193
FACTORY 7117
SHOW ROOMS 2-1193

No. 1183

No. 2034

**MATCHLESS
QUALITY MIZNER
PRODUCTS**

There are products that
only Mizner Industries
can offer.

Unusual tile and pot-
tery.

Perfectly reproduced
period furniture.

Artistic stone.

Extraordinary wrought
iron.

Beautiful leaded and
stained glass.

Simple or elaborate
ceilings.

Complete paneled
rooms.

Durable bronze sash.

And many other excep-
tional products.

No. 1185

Many of the furnishings and architectural features of the Cloister Inn were provided by the factories of Mizner Industries, operating out of West Palm Beach. *Boca Raton Historical Society.*

costly hotels in the state." The company also completed 350 walnut-framed, straight-back chairs with leather seats and backs, as well as two antique cupboards for the dining room. Finally, the article claimed that Mizner personally handled the interior decoration of the hotel and used some of the most valuable of his own antiques in the lobby and other large public rooms, making it "one of the most distinguished in Florida."

Even before the Cloister Inn opened, Mizner gave two parties in Boca Raton during the 1925 holiday season. On Christmas Day he entertained a large group of former clients and friends from Palm Beach at dinner in the "Salamanca" room of the Cloister. A photograph shows that the unfinished cloister itself served as the setting for "the opening of the social season in Boca Raton and is the harbinger of the many exclusive dinners and parties that are to follow." This was the first hotel event under the management of the Ritz-Carlton system, which had agreed to manage the Cloister Inn. On New Year's Eve, Mizner held a dinner dance at the Administration Buildings for an even

On Christmas Day 1925, Mizner hosted a party for his Palm Beach friends at the not-quite-finished Cloister Inn. Notice the unfinished walls at right. *Boca Raton Historical Society.*

larger group, though many of the same people attended both events. The evening's entertainment culminated at midnight with the "Grand March à la Mizner." Even the *New York Times* mentioned the party in an article on "New Year's at Palm Beach."

Just before the hotel held its official opening, Mizner publicity released the news that Boca Raton planned to spend $1 million in city improvements in cooperation with the development company. These included a large, two-story city hall designed by Mizner and constructed on lots donated by the company; the building of a new police headquarters, fire hall and school; the erection of a new drawbridge across the Intracoastal Waterway at Palmetto Park Road; and the widening and curbing of all major streets. Calling Boca Raton the "Cinderella of Florida" and Addison Mizner its fairy godfather, Mayor J.G. Brown promised "to stand with and by [Mizner Development] in every way in our power."

The hotel, now known as the Ritz-Carlton Cloister Inn and managed by Gustav Tott, formerly of the Atlantic City Ritz-Carlton, opened on February 6, 1926, with an informal dinner attended by nearly 350 members of Palm Beach society. One account said the names inscribed in the great Spanish leather guest book rivaled "the social registers of two continents" and called the dinner one of the outstanding social events of the season. During the "Lucullan repast," served on china in the Spanish colors of red and yellow by red-coated and gold-braided waiters, Alexander P. Moore, former ambassador to Spain, in recognizing the beauty of the Cloister Inn, said its charm "is as radiant as anything there is in Spain" and paid tribute to Mizner as the "Michael Angelo of America."

Perched at the edge of Lake Boca Raton, the new Ritz-Carlton Cloister Inn was a low, rambling building with red-tile roofs and a tower projecting height. Mizner designed his one-hundred-room hotel with three floors of guest rooms on the western and southern sides of a great court. Its namesake cloister enclosed the lake side of the court on the east, joining the guest rooms, the lounge and a columned loggia that filled in its north end. The lounge and dining room also overlooked a lakefront terrace north of the building. The tower, modeled on the Giralda of Seville, rose three stories over the hotel wing at the northwest corner of the court. A two-story northern wing contained the kitchen and other service facilities and around sixty-six rooms for the hotel's staff. To the north of this wing, a large garage provided rooms for chauffeurs on its second floor.

A Spanish convent of the eleventh century furnished Mizner's inspiration for the hotel. Entry was through a porch formed by a wide Romanesque arch supported by two short columns with ornate capitals. The entrance surround rose to the base of the windows on the third floor and contained Queen Isabella's shield on one side and King Ferdinand's on the other. Mizner publicity claimed the high wooden entrance doors came from the University of Salamanca and were four hundred years old. The door surround, made by Mizner Industries of cast stone, had two narrow columns on pedestals with the same capitals as the entrance arch. The columns supported a pediment and a molded coat of arms. The lobby was forty-foot square and two stories high, with a hanging pecky cypress balcony supported by narrow beams on two sides on the second floor. Bright white plaster walls, a wood-beamed ceiling and a polished red-tile floor completed the austere "convent" decor. Wood-framed leather straight and arm chairs, dark wooden chests and writing tables and pots of palms furnished the space. Mizner placed one of his usual staircases with elegant low risers on the east side of the lobby opposite the entry.

This image is of the west façade, or the main entrance to the Cloister Inn, circa 1926. Today, this is the eastern wing of the Boca Raton Resort & Club's historic section. *Photo by Ray B. Dame, Boca Raton Historical Society.*

The beauty of the Cloister Inn is revealed in this lakefront view of the hotel, circa 1926. The section at left was demolished to make way for the tower in 1967. *Photo by Ray B. Dame, Boca Raton Historical Society.*

The main entrance to the Cloister Inn was through a Romanesque arch "reminiscent of the entrance gate to the University of Salamanca," according to one newspaper report. *Photo by Ray B. Dame, Boca Raton Historical Society.*

The lobby of the Cloister Inn featured bright white plaster walls, a wood-beamed ceiling and a polished red floor with austere "convent" decor. *Photo by Ray B. Dame, Boca Raton Historical Society.*

Also on the east wall, another high wooden door opened onto the loggia with its six colossal columns supporting the beamed ceiling. The thirty- by fifty-foot loggia overlooked the court and provided an entry into the dining room, smoking room, lounge and cloister. The waxed cement tile floor in both the loggia and cloister might provide a hint to Mizner's financial difficulties as he completed the hotel. A plain pointed arch surround and another wooden door provided entrance to the thirteenth-century dining hall. Flanking the door were two windows with ornate Gothic surrounds glazed with softly stained green, yellow and rose glass. The dining hall, forty by eighty-four feet, rose thirty-five feet to five massive masonry Gothic arches supporting a wooden-beamed ceiling. Mizner said he took as his model for the room the refectory of the fifteenth-century hospital at Vich in Catalonia. He furnished the room with the walnut-framed and nail-studded leather chairs from his factory, wrought-iron chandeliers and standing candle holders from his blacksmith shops and a waxed red-octagonal floor tile from Las Manos.

Mizner placed a small smoking room between the dining hall and the lounge. He furnished this room with the Papa Mizner chair with cushioned upholstery designed and manufactured in his furniture factory as an answer to the client who claimed all antique Spanish chairs were uncomfortable. He named a smaller version for women the Mama Mizner chair. The lounge, sometimes called the ballroom, projected over the lake. Like the loggia, it had massive wooden trestles supporting its ceiling. The fireplace, with a cast-stone mantle from Mizner Industries, was so huge that "a man might walk up-right." Shields with clusters of brightly colored flags decorated the walls, and Papa Mizner chairs, upholstered sofas and dark wooden furniture completed the sparse decor.

Locals Harriette Gates and Helen Howard enjoy tea in the loggia of the inn, circa 1926. *Boca Raton Historical Society.*

The dining hall was modeled after a refectory of the fifteenth-century hospital at Vich in Catalonia. It was furnished with items constructed at the Mizner Industries factories in West Palm Beach. *Photo by Ray B. Dame, Boca Raton Historical Society.*

On the north wall, arched doors opened onto the terrace and dance floor, and on the south wall, onto the cloister. The cloister bordered Lake Boca Raton and "is such as the priests of old trod with sandaled feet." The almost triangular-shaped "fantastic" capitals had crudely carved grotesque figures and animals. Rattan chairs from Mizner's workshops furnished the area, as did plants in glazed Las Manos pots.

The guest rooms were at the end of the cloister and could also be entered from a hallway off the lobby. Early Mizner publicity said that the architect planned each in a style of a famous old-world room with varied color schemes. When the hotel opened, the bedrooms had "intentionally" been made very simple, "with something of the old quality of the severe beauty to be found in convents and monasteries." According to one account, Mizner actually used brown terrazzo for the guest room floors, creamy whitewash for the walls and a "curious tomato color" for the doors, shutters and bedspreads. The Las Manos–made guest room lamps were plain cement in the shape of wine amphoras standing on wrought-iron bases. Mizner publicity used to its advantage the necessity of furnishing the Cloister Inn modestly, saying that the decor "harks back to earlier Monastic days…and reeks of the atmosphere of early religious orders in its simplicity."

Everyone who saw the Ritz-Carlton Cloister Inn praised its architecture. The critic and historian Giles Edgerton, writing in the April 1926 edition of *Arts & Decoration*, asked

The lounge, or ballroom, of the Cloister Inn had massive wooden rafters and a fireplace with a cast-stone mantle, so huge "a man might walk up-right." *Photo by Ray B. Dame, Boca Raton Historical Society.*

The cloister of the Cloister Inn featured columns with capitals decorated with grotesque animals and figures. Local legend has it that they were installed upside down—clearly untrue upon close examination. *Photo by Ray B. Dame, Boca Raton Historical Society.*

Right: This view from the cloister of the Cloister Inn shows the hotel's original tower and the "Mizner Loggia." Note the elaborate column capitals and the future site of the Cloister Garden. *Photo by Ray B. Dame, Boca Raton Historical Society*.

Below: The guest rooms of the Cloister Inn were intentionally simple, reflecting the "severe beauty to be found in convents and monasteries." *Photo by Ray B. Dame, Boca Raton Historical Society*.

"what could make forms of wood, or stone, or stucco so beautiful that they trouble the imagination?" While he pointed out that the Cloister Inn had every modern comfort and convenience, its picturesque beauty came from its mediaeval inspiration and, as such, it "exhales an atmosphere of beautiful, austere simplicity in outline and arrangement." Ida Tarbell, who visited the hotel shortly after it opened, wrote in *Florida Architecture of Addison Mizner* that the 'Cloister was simple to severity in its whole yet rich in delights." For Mizner, the ultimate accolade for the Cloister Inn came from the widow of Stanford White, the architect he most admired. She said: "Addison Mizner is the foremost genius of the age. Since Stanford White, there has been no one with such exquisite sense of artistry. This building is superb."

The opening of the Ritz-Carlton Cloister Inn allowed Harry Reichenbach's publicity department to focus new attention on the Mizner development. The unquestioned beauty of the hotel demonstrated the architect's vision for the entire city. His dinner guests from Palm Beach society, the show business world and the British aristocracy proved a continuing interest in the development by the fashionable. Unfortunately, no matter how hard Mizner's publicity department worked, the opening of the Ritz-Carlton Cloister Inn failed to save the Boca Raton development. Even before the hotel opened, the Florida land boom had ended.

As the Mizner Development Corporation's financial problems deepened, its publicity department continued to emphasize both through advertisements and press releases those projects that promoted the continued value of the Boca Raton property and the leaders of society and American business who supported Mizner's vision. One recurring theme heralded Boca Raton as a sportsman's paradise. While other developments might have one golf course, Mizner's company planned at least three. Donald J. Ross, one of the country's best-known golf course architects, designed the Cloister's course, while William J. Flynn, who also had an international reputation, planned two more for Ritz-Carlton Park in far western Boca Raton. Of the two Flynn-designed courses, the one north of Camino Real would serve the guests of the oceanfront hotel; the southern course was "reserved and restricted." The large Lake Esmarelda on the south course, the site of the clubhouse, would be "one of the most attractive artificial inland marine bodies in Florida" and well worth the cost of $50,000 as it also served as a hazard for the golf course.

Equestrian sports also played a prominent role in the city as Mizner promised to build polo fields, and later, because of the interest of "fashionable persons," he had bridle paths laid out and thirty-seven saddle horses brought down from Tennessee by the development's road builder. Several press releases also mentioned the founding of a hunt club and the laying out of a steeplechase course. The publicity department said that if plans for a race course, with a grandstand designed by Mizner, materialized, Mrs. W.K. Vanderbilt Jr. planned to establish her winter stable in the resort, and many others might do the same, making Boca Raton the winter counterpoint to Saratoga.

Mizner also remembered those interested in water sports. The company promised to dredge the inlet to allow large yachts to enter Lake Boca Raton, and its literature always mentioned the ability to dock at the Cloister Inn. Other press releases boasted of the planned sixty-one miles of canals leaving no part of the development untouched by waterways and making Boca Raton truly "the Venice of America." As the Ritz-Carlton

Here Captain Ernest F. Carter (left), C.E. Karstrom (center) and a man identified as McKenzie (right) take on the eighteenth hole at one of the two courses at the Cloister Inn, 1926. *Boca Raton Historical Society*.

The Boca Raton Hunt Club, yet another attempt to attract high society to the young community, was organized in January 1927, with fifty-five members. Here they pose at the northwest corner of the Cloister Inn. *Boca Raton Historical Society*.

Cloister Inn had no pool, the company proudly pointed to the new Mizner-designed bath houses on the beach. The "Spanish" cabanas "in riotous colors and with complete equipment radiated an aura of comfort and ease reminiscent of the Lido." The Cloister Inn served lunch and tea on the beach. The hotel decided to lease the bath houses by the season and allow the renters "to place their coats of arms over the doorways."

While sports filled the day, Mizner also planned evening entertainment. The company often mentioned concerts and impromptu recitals held at the Cloister Inn or in its various sales offices. Al Jolson and Irving Berlin figured prominently in press releases as interested in Boca Raton. Just before the Cloister opened, several articles told of Mizner's younger brother, Wilson, the vice president of the development company, assuming management of the amusement plans for the resort. A successful playwright with many friends in the business, his experience in the New York theatrical world made him the best person to negotiate for "the most pretentious successes of Broadway." Wilson also planned a nightclub called the Pirate Ship Cabaret anchored in Lake Boca Raton. The cabaret, to seat four hundred, would serve French cuisine at dinner and Spanish at the after-theatre supper. Reports claimed that Wilson purchased boats and barges in Baltimore for use by his brother in designing the pirate ship.

Publicity releases continued to cite land sales statistics, such as the $680,000 worth of lots purchased on December 19, 1925, in the Palm Beach office alone, saying that December was usually a "dull" month. Articles constantly mentioned total sales of over $30 million from late May, when Plat One first went on the market, until the end of the year. The same releases played up the "they are buying to build" theme. Stories circulated about the residents of Spanish Village, the construction of houses in what later became Floresta, where one of Mizner's older brothers, the Reverend Henry Mizner, would live, as well as Mizner Development Corporation executives whose offices were moved to the Administration Building, and of new houses erected by West Palm Beach builder Hansell Hall. These colorful bungalows of five or six rooms were in the Spanish style. The Drucker Construction Company announced a $100,000 building on Camino Real, diagonally across from the Administration Buildings, with ten stores and eight apartments designed by Mizner in a style similar to London's Burlington Arcade. Drucker also proposed a hundred-unit subdivision in the area directly south of the Cloister Inn, with ten houses designed by Mizner to be built immediately.

Although the development company realized the need to appeal to the individual buyers of lots, it continued to stress the fashionableness of the project. The interest in the exclusive Distrito de Boca Raton became a recurring theme for its publicity. Countess Millicent Salm, the Standard Oil heiress and tabloid sensation because of her divorce and custody battle with the count, received approval to purchase the first Distrito lot of 150 oceanfront feet for $150,000. One article reported total sales for opening month of almost $700,000 and claimed that this would have reached well over a million except the "stringent social restrictions" placed on the property caused the committee in charge to return several large checks. Those ultimately approved gave the Distrito the status of "rendezvous of the elite of the world."

To help reassure "the investors in Boca Raton," Mizner sent each lot owner a letter in January, just before the Cloister Inn opened, that admitted problems in the Florida real

Addison Mizner poses with his brother, Wilson, and actress Marie Dressler, who was recruited to help promote the Boca Raton development project. *Boca Raton Historical Society.*

estate market, though it divorced Boca Raton from these troubles. While mentioning all the projects the company had completed in the city, the letter also pointed out the over $30 million in sales as proof of the project's worth. To reassure those who purchased lots hoping to resell at a profit, Mizner claimed $2.3 million in resold lots "with profits to the original purchaser in every case." This outstanding record was a result of the "remarkable progress" made in completing the promised improvements.

The ultimate objective of the publicity was to sell lots in the development. Hoping to restart stalled sales, the company held an auction of oceanfront lots on the patio of the Administration Buildings. The fifty-foot lots in northern Boca Raton attracted about two thousand people to the auction, which sold the entire allotment in two days. Although Mizner publicity claimed this proved that "the realty market has returned to a normal, healthy base," unfortunately, the sale netted only about $250,000.

Throughout the 1926 winter season, Mizner's publicity also told of the popularity of the Ritz-Carlton Cloister Inn. Almost daily, lists of well-known socialites "motoring" to the Cloister from Palm Beach or Miami for lunch or tea appeared in area newspapers. One article mentioned the "magical delights" of the Cloister and claimed "pilgrimages that were made for art in the olden days are reenacted today with the Cloister as the goal." Most of the news releases about visitors centered on the hotel and its popularity, though some also pointed out how much the Boca Raton development impressed the visitor.

There were many notable visitors. Soon after the Cloister opened, Charles Ritz, son of the founder of the Ritz-Carlton system, and his new wife arrived for a belated honeymoon. Sergeant Alvin C. York, World War I hero, stopped at the hotel. Clarence Darrow, who defended the cause of evolution, was a guest at a party, as was Joseph E. Widener, "well known Palm Beach and Philadelphia sportsman." John Ringling, of circus fame, came across the state to stay at the Cloister, and a number of well-known authors attended dinners and parties at the hotel. The movie stars Richard Barthlemess and Bebe Daniels were early hotel guests, and opera stars Madame Amelita Galli-Curei, Madame Frances Alda and Rafael Diaz were often visitors. The celebrity most associated with the Cloister Inn during its opening season was Marie Dressler. Mizner installed the popular comedienne, who came to Florida to sell real estate, as the hotel's hostess. One source said "she had the time of her life," and everyone called her the "Duchess of Boca Raton."

Unfortunately, Harry Reichenbach's publicity and the sale of a few oceanfront lots failed to resurrect the boom. By early spring 1926, new land sales had ended. To continue to build the project Mizner's company promised for Boca Raton, he needed these sales. Moreover, by May, the second installment was due from those who had purchased the first block of lots with 20 percent down payments. Many who had no money for a second payment and had planned early profitable sales now found no buyers. Others, fearing their lots might become worthless given the declining value of Boca Raton real estate, decided to cut their losses. Mizner had counted on these installments to continue construction and make payments on the development company's mortgages.

Also in May, various contractors, unable to collect on their contracts, filed liens against the company. Mizner held on by taking loans from the Palm Beach National and other local banks, often controlled by members of his board of directors. Unfortunately, by late June, many of these banks had failed, turning a bad situation into an impossible one. Then, in July, it looked as if the Dawes brothers of Chicago might save the insolvent company. Their Central Equities Corporation, headed by Rufus Dawes, promised to bail Mizner out with a large loan in return for controlling interest in the development company. Another brother, Charles Dawes, at the time vice president of the United States, was instrumental in facilitating the arrangement, which kept Mizner as figurehead president and in control of architectural development. The hope that the Dawes brothers' money might save the project ended on September 18, 1926, when a powerful hurricane struck Miami. After inflicting much damage to property and great loss of life, it swept across the state to Lake Okeechobee, where as many as three hundred more died. Although Boca Raton suffered little physical damage, the hurricane became the coup de grâce for the land boom in the state. After it hit, no hope remained of reviving sales or building.

According to Raymond B. Vickers in *Panic in Paradise: Florida's Banking Crash of 1926*, the Dawes brothers never attempted to save the Boca Raton development. With controlling interest in the Mizner company, they seized the contracts of the lot buyers, filed mortgages on land owned by the company and placed liens on its equipment, securing for themselves "the unencumbered assets of Mizner Development Corporation, leaving its debts and other liabilities to the unsecured creditors." A later investigation showed that the Central Equities Corporation had held $13 million in Mizner sales contracts as security for a $100,000 loan to the company and had applied collections on the sales contracts toward payment of the loan.

The Ritz-Carlton Cloister Inn opened for its second season on January 17, 1927. No longer the smart destination for the fashionable of Palm Beach or Miami, it tried appealing to Boca Raton lot owners, offering a 25 percent reduction in rates during the season. In March, the company was sued for $50,552 by three New York men who charged that it was insolvent and had engaged in "false and fraudulent" sales practices. Mizner answered for the company by saying he had never heard of the petitioners and that the company continued to receive new money. Then, in April, Harry and Ethel Chesebro, Boca Raton pioneers, sued to foreclose on thirty-two acres of land that included the Cloister Inn. The Chesebros said the company had stopped paying on the $115,000 purchase price and asked for a lien on the property so it might be sold. They claimed that Mizner owed them $75,000 in principal and interest and $3,000 in attorney's fees. In June, the Riddle Engineering Company filed a bankruptcy petition, attacking the Dawes brothers for unlawful depletion of Mizner company assets. Riddle claimed the company owed him $30,760. In July, the Mizner Development Corporation was adjudicated bankrupt. Vicker says the bankruptcy left 173 creditors with $4,192,000 in unsecured claims. After a three-year wait, the bankruptcy court award the creditors .001 percent on their claims. Carl Riddle received $30.76.

In October 1927, J.D. Gedney, a New York attorney, was the successful bidder in the bankruptcy sale of the Cloister Inn and other Mizner properties. The bid of $5,000, which included assumption of outstanding obligations, was the only blanket offer made for all the buildings and the fifteen thousand acres of land. Max Specktor of West Palm Beach purchased the Cloister Inn's furnishings at an auction held a week earlier for $28,000. In mid-October, the referee in bankruptcy rejected both sale prices as insufficient considering the worth of the properties. In a second round of bidding in early November, Gedney offered $71,500 for the Cloister Inn, its furnishings, the rest of the Mizner properties and assumption of all outstanding obligations. The referee in bankruptcy approved the sale on November 19, 1927. By this time, Gedney had revealed that he acted for Clarence H. Geist, a Philadelphia utilities magnate and former member of Mizner's board of directors.

Addison Mizner's development was doomed to failure from the very beginning; the boom peaked just as he entered the market. Still, he attempted to build his dream. The "gloriously beautiful" and architecturally perfect hotel with "magnificent furnishings" that combined old-world charm with new-world convenience became the Boca Raton Resort & Club and stands as a tribute to that dream. Considering the length of his active building time in Boca Raton, starting in the summer of 1925 and ending twelve months later when the Central Equities Company took over direction of his company, he accomplished a great deal: the Ritz-Carlton Cloister Inn, the Administration Buildings, the original plan for the town hall, houses in Spanish Village, Old Floresta and those of the Drucker Company. These left an architectural legacy that Boca Raton would draw upon in the 1980s to create its second "Mizner period."

Chapter 2

The Boca Raton Club

Newspaper reports in November 1927 told of Clarence H. Geist's plan to establish a private golf club in Boca Raton on the former Mizner property. As in the case of Addison Mizner, over the years many myths have grown around Geist and his club. First and foremost among them is the reason for establishing a new club: the membership committee of Palm Beach's exclusive Everglades Club blackballed his application for admission because he was loud, vulgar and crude. In retaliation, he proposed a Boca Raton Club so exclusive "that members of the Everglades would be excluded." Moreover, he planned a club "so magnificent that the Everglades would look like a tar paper shack community." Theodore Pratt, a local author who published several articles in national magazines and the short booklet *The Story of Boca Raton* in the 1950s, said that this legend was only true in "spirit." Geist's friends never proposed him for membership to the Everglades "because what would happen was obvious and no one cared to be embarrassed." This caused Geist to create his club "to both have a place where he could be 'czar' and because he regarded it as a good business investment."

In reality, Geist was a member of the Everglades Club, a close friend of Paris Singer, its owner, and lived on a private street created by Singer on its grounds. Moreover, when the Bath and Tennis Club, the second of the exclusive Palm Beach clubs of the 1920s opened, Geist became a charter member. Finally, his nephew, Bradley Geist, who lived with the Geist family for eleven years in Philadelphia, Palm Beach and Boca Raton, emphasized that "he was not coarse" and was "generous to a fault." He liked to joke and kid and had a merry time with his many friends. Geist, "this most delightful man," also served as Bradley's best man when he married in 1935.

Geist, an enthusiastic golfer and a longtime winter visitor to Palm Beach, founded the Seaview Golf Club near Atlantic City, New Jersey, in 1914. The club, situated on five hundred acres of land, had an eighteen-hole course considered one of the best in the country and a large clubhouse-hotel. President Warren G. Harding and New York Governor Alfred E. Smith were among the notables entertained at the club, which

Clarence Geist, who purchased the Cloister Inn in 1927, is shown with his wife, Florence, sometime in the 1930s. *Boca Raton Historical Society.*

Clarence Geist, President Warren Harding, Senator Joseph Frelinghusen and an unidentified man pose in front of Geist's Seaview Golf Club in New Jersey. *Photo by Atlantic Foto Service, Boca Raton Historical Society.*

Geist financed and owned and whose members included some of the nation's leading industrialists and wealthiest men. In March 1924, Geist told a reporter for the *Palm Beach Daily News* that some of his Seaview members asked him to build a similar club in Palm Beach for the winter months. Although he searched for a suitable piece of land to place a four-hundred-room clubhouse-hotel and two eighteen-hole golf courses, he abandoned his plans because the Florida land boom had made it impossible to find a large enough tract. Buying the Cloister Inn and the other properties of Mizner Development Corporation solved that problem.

By 1927, Geist could well afford to finance a second seasonal golf club. Born on a farm near LaPorte, Indiana, in 1866, as a young man he traveled to the West, where he bought and sold livestock. Always ambitious and a hard worker, he lived largely in the saddle for the next four or five years before going to Chicago because "no one in the west had any money, and I discovered the fact that I could not make any money where there wasn't any." After working on the Rock Island Railroad and then selling real estate for a few years, he became associated with Charles and Rufus Dawes in the development of gas and electric utilities companies. They retained their interests in the companies until the late 1920s, when they sold out to Samuel Insull.

In 1905, Geist married Florence Hewitt of Philadelphia and came east to live. He continued to buy utility companies and owned the Indianapolis Water Company and the Philadelphia Suburban Water Company, which supplied water to forty-nine towns near the city. At the same time, he developed the new club in Boca Raton, he sold a number of his gas and electric utilities for stock in the United Gas Improvement Company and joined its board of directors. The *New York Times* claimed he owned 400,000 shares of the company and was its largest stockholder.

Newspaper accounts of the sale of the Mizner property said it represented approximately a $7 million deal, including a payment of $71,500 and the assumption of all mortgages and obligations of the development company. The transaction involved all Mizner properties east of the Florida East Coast Railway to the ocean and included the Cloister Inn and golf course, the two administration buildings and approximately fifteen hundred acres of land. From the first, Geist said he planned to remodel the entire property into a "sportsman's paradise" similar to his Seaview club. His new club, though specifically devoted to golf, would also have provision for tennis, yachting, swimming and riding. On an early November visit to Boca Raton, he brought golf course architects Toomey and Flynn, who he said would lay out and reconstruct the Cloister course for the winter season. He also said he planned to enlarge the inn and add swimming pavilions as soon as possible.

This view, taken from atop the main entrance to the Boca Raton Club, shows the west wing of the club under construction in 1929. Note the Toomey and Flynn–designed golf course to the south of Camino Real. *Boca Raton Historical Society.*

Geist also announced that he proposed "to run this new project along entirely different lines…no one connected with the old organization will have anything to do under the new regime," though he promised to protect all property owners and give them clear titles to their land in the future. He added that the purchase of the Mizner land proved his absolute belief in Florida and its future: "As long as Florida sunshine continues to shine, people will come to Florida." Prominent local businessmen were enthusiastic about the sale and Geist's plans for the property, declaring it the best Florida news for months.

As architects for the additions to the Cloister Inn, Geist turned to the New York firm of Schultze and Weaver. Leonard Schultze and S. Fullerton Weaver formed the firm in 1921 and quickly became known for their hotels and large office buildings. Of the two partners, Schultze served as the architect, while Weaver, an engineer and builder, ran the company. Schultze, born in Chicago in 1878, studied architecture in New York at a Beaux-Arts program of the Metropolitan Museum of Art under the mentorship of Emmanuel L. Masqueray, a French-born graduate of the École des Beaux Arts in Paris who came to New York in 1887. In 1900, Schultze joined the firm of Warren & Wetmore, becoming chief of design for Grand Central Terminal and executive in charge of its construction. He remained with Warren & Wetmore until he formed his firm with Weaver. Born in Philadelphia in 1879, Weaver graduated in civil engineering from the University of Pennsylvania and formed his own construction company, becoming a pioneer in the building of Park Avenue apartment houses on the leasehold grounds of the New York Central Railroad.

Schultze and Weaver had immediate success, with the Park Lane, Waldorf-Astoria and Sherry-Netherlands Hotels among their New York City projects. The firm's work was well known in South Florida by 1927. It had designed the Biltmore Hotel for Coral Gables, the Miami Daily News Tower on Biscayne Boulevard and the Roney Plaza Hotel across the bay in Miami Beach. All three buildings had towers modeled from the Giralda in Seville. In 1926, the firm designed a massive downtown Miami office building and received the commission to plan a new Breakers Hotel in Palm Beach after the old wooden hotel had been destroyed in a spectacular fire in 1925.

Since the Beaux-Arts-trained Schultze worked in many architectural styles, he was comfortable with the Mediterranean architecture of the Cloister Inn and incorporated the inn and many of Mizner's design motifs into the new building. Entrance to the club was from a new 340-foot-square courtyard, approached by a royal palm–lined drive from Camino Real. The Cloister Inn enclosed the courtyard on the east and half of its south side, while the new clubhouse formed the other sides. The lavishly landscaped courtyard contained a circular driveway with a large tiled fountain in its center capped by a statue, *The Slave Girl*, by Italian-born sculptor Ettore Pellegatta. Geist also commissioned a colorful tile mural designed by John W. Haynes entitled *East Meets West* that created a centerpiece for the courtyard gate. Across from the wrought-iron gates, the architects placed the new main entrance to the club though a porte-cochère on the north side of the courtyard. This section's six-story height was capped at both ends by eight-story-high towers echoing Mizner's design for the Cloister Inn tower. On the west side of the courtyard, the height stepped down from five floors to four for the major part of the wing. Balconies and window surrounds again played upon Mizner's various motifs. The new construction added a total of three hundred guest rooms. A final homage to the Palm Beach architect came with the copy of the great Romanesque arch of the Cloister's entrance to serve as the entrance to the men's locker rooms on the western façade, facing the golf course.

Schultze and Weaver retained all of Mizner's public rooms, though they added a large dining hall to serve the greatly enlarged number of guests. From the first, because of its plan and size, it was called the Cathedral Dining Room. Located on the lakefront, its impressive door opened upon the dance terrace, though in inclement weather it could be accessed through a hall on the north side of Mizner's old dining room. That room, which now served as a comfortable lounge, received a new fireplace, with a cast-stone mantel, on its north wall and a new entry from the Schultze and Weaver lobby. New, greatly enlarged kitchens, staff dining rooms and laundry and utility rooms replaced Mizner's north wing. Also, as part of the northern section of the hotel, there was a new indoor swimming pool with locker room facilities for both men and women.

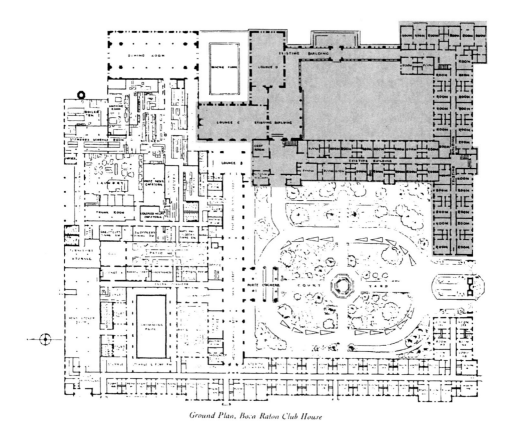

Ground Plan, Boca Raton Club House

This plan shows the ground floor of the Boca Raton Club; the main courtyard is at lower right. The grayed area represents the original portions of the Cloister Inn, incorporated into the Schultze and Weaver design. *Boca Raton Historical Society.*

Right: This 1930s view shows the fountain at the center of the Camino Real "roundabout" and original "boulevard" into the Boca Raton Club. *Photo by Townsend, Boca Raton Historical Society.*

Below: This photo was taken from atop the main lobby of the Boca Raton Club, looking southeast. Notice the undeveloped Estates section and inlet in the far left ground. *Photo by Clifford Norton, Boca Raton Historical Society.*

Above: Italian-born artist Ettore Pellegatta designed the statue and fountain at the center of the main courtyard of the Boca Raton Club. *The Slave Girl* was supposedly modeled after his wife, Lina. *Photo by Clifford Norton, Boca Raton Historical Society.*

Below: The rear of the main gate of the Boca Raton Club, visible to departing guests, featured a tile mosaic depicting *East Meets West*, designed by John W. Haymes. *Photo by Edgar C. Schmid, Boca Raton Raton Historical Society.*

Boca Raton motorcycle cop Eugene Carter stands with groundskeeper Clyde Miller on the road running through the golf course on the west side of the Boca Raton Club, 1932. *Boca Raton Historical Society.*

The Cathedral Dining Room of the Boca Raton Club was essentially a separate structure on the edge of Lake Boca Raton, overlooking a dance floor and patio. *Photo by Frank E. Geisler, Boca Raton Historical Society.*

Above: The aptly named Cathedral Dining Room included gold-leafed columns, a polychrome coffered ceiling and gigantic Venetian chandeliers. *Photo by Frank E. Geisler, Boca Raton Historical Society.*

Left: The former dining room of Mizner's Cloister Inn became a lounge under Geist's ownership. This photo reveals the large baronial fireplace added by Schultze and Weaver. *Boca Raton Historical Society.*

In early July 1928, the Seaboard and Southern Corporation of Jacksonville received the $2 million contract for the new club. With the end of the Land Boom, building had almost ceased in southeastern Florida. When the company awarded many subcontracts to local businesses, it gave area construction workers their first chance of employment in many months. Newspapers called the three-hundred-room addition to the Cloister Inn the largest project on the Florida East Coast. Geist's organization said construction would begin in August, with completion scheduled for October 1929. At the same time, Geist announced the renovation of the Administration Buildings for use as a golf clubhouse during the 1928–29 season, the dredging of Lake Boca Raton and the construction of an ocean inlet with jetties. To decorate the new club, Geist appointed the New York and Palm Beach art dealer Ohan S. Berberyan.

To ensure that he retained control of the old Mizner Development property, Geist formed the Boca Raton Syndicate with $1 million capital, of which he subscribed $595,000 of the total, while twenty-nine other members subscribed between $5,000 and $25,000. In turn, the syndicate controlled the Boca Raton Club and the Spanish River Land Company, which was formed to manage the Mizner land not associated with the club. Geist proposed that seven hundred club members pay $5,000 for memberships and as a bonus receive fifty shares of stock in the land company. Of the $3.5 million raised,

The lobby area surrounding the grand staircase represents a transition between the Schultze and Weaver–designed lobby, in the background, and the original Cloister Inn lobby, out of view at left. *Boca Raton Historical Society.*

The entrance to the new Boca Raton Club lounge, formerly the dining room at the Cloister Inn, was at the east end of the main lobby, adjacent the grand staircase. *Boca Raton Historical Society.*

$1 million paid for the initial cost of the club property and the rest for improvements, which included a second golf course, a nine-hole practice course, a swimming pavilion and a casino on the beach for ocean bathing. The $5,000 fee gave each member a proprietary interest in the club, which then charged modest dues of $100 a year. The club's brochure pointed out that the land company purchased these properties "at very advantageous prices," and their value greatly exceeded the cost to the club. Moreover, the sale of the properties retained by the land company would be profitable, and club members would participate because of their stock ownership.

In April 1929, before the completion of the new club building, Geist invited Boca Raton's citizens to a dinner at the Cloister Inn, where, in a rambling speech, he outlined his plans for the club and his expectations for the town. Claiming Boca Raton had only "two pests," the mosquito and politics, he proposed to eliminate both: the mosquito, by doing away with standing water; and politics, by making all elected officials except the town clerk serve without salaries. Saying he planned to develop the Mizner property and bring in more winter residents to build houses, which in turn would build the town, he called for low taxes that everyone could pay. This, he claimed, would keep the treasury full and allow the necessary improvements to attract even more winter visitors. "Bring the people here for the winter, get their money while they are here and you wont have to do a lot of work throughout the hot weather of the summer." If he built a "splendid community of houses," the people who lived in Boca Raton had to cooperate with him. Without this cooperation, he threatened to run the club and forget about the town and its development. The cooperation he asked for: hold elections in February so the new winter residents could vote, beautify the town and build a water plant. In a lighter vein, he said people were killed by three things: "first is bad water, the second bad whisky, and the third good whisky." Claiming always to have the interests of Boca Raton at heart, he said he did not come to take anything away. "The sun, the ocean and the climate is something that no one can take away from this town…Everything that I do here must be bringing something to Boca Raton." Although still threatening to withdraw behind the club walls if the citizens of Boca Raton refused to cooperate with him, he also gave each citizen five shares of the Spanish River Land Company so they might participate in the success of his plans. The talk and the shares seemed to work.

The Boca Raton town commissioners realized the importance of the club to its citizens and showed a willingness to work with Geist from the beginning. Sometimes referred to as "water boy" because of his ownership of utility companies, Geist believed that "good water" was the "foundation of every community." Although the town's debts from the land boom days found it unable to make payments on "Old Betsy," its fire engine, even before Geist's talk, at a late August 1928 meeting, the commission agreed to a new pumping station and water treatment plant financed by a loan from the hotel after its voters approved it by a thirty to twelve margin. In June 1929, Geist asked for the addition of a plant to purify and soften the water before the club opened. The commission hastily agreed and, declaring public health and safety at stake, passed an emergency measure to borrow the necessary money by issuing $55,000 in bonds so construction could start as soon as possible. The plant, built on Palmetto Park Road at the site of the current city hall, served Boca Raton until 1956. When constructed, the town contained probably less than 150 voters, though its lime-softened water treatment plant equaled those of Miami and West Palm Beach. Clarence Geist received his "good water."

To ensure that this type of loyalty continued, the town commission voted itself out of existence. In March 1929, the commission asked the state legislature to approve a new town charter, which called for the election of a mayor, five council members and a clerk. When the legislature approved it, these officers were first elected in July 1929, with terms ending on the last day of February 1931. In succeeding elections on the third Tuesday of February, Geist would be in town to "oversee" them, and more importantly, the people who had built winter houses could vote.

When Geist, his daughter Elizabeth and his nephew Bradley arrived in Boca Raton on January 7, 1930, they found a completed clubhouse and several guests who had checked in before them. Even though Geist had leased his Golf View Road house for the season, the party had stopped in Palm Beach because there were as yet no station facilities in Boca Raton for his private railroad car. He had acted to solve this problem by shifting Dixie Highway to the east and giving the land between the road and tracks, just north of Camino Real, to the Florida East Coast Railway for a new station. This station, designed in the Spanish style by FEC architect Chester G. Henninger, was landscaped in June 1930 and ready for Geist's arrival the following season.

Geist loaned the Town of Boca Raton money to build a new water treatment plant to serve the citizens, as well as guests at the new Boca Raton Club. *Boca Raton Historical Society.*

Geist gave land to the Florida East Coast Railway for a passenger station suitable for his new hotel guests. The station, designed by Chester Henninger, opened in June 1930. *Boca Raton Historical Society.*

In January 1930, the Geist party, which took up club residency in a palatial suite of rooms on the sixth floor, did so with no formal ceremony marking the club's opening or Geist's arrival, though in following years, when his private car reached the new station, the hotel orchestra and staff and the town's citizens were all in attendance. Although the new swimming pavilion and tennis courts south of the club were ready for members when it opened, the club beach contained only twenty-four temporary cabanas, and the new southern golf course was still incomplete.

During the first season, work continued on the inlet and the bulkheading of the lake, and it was decided to build a permanent bathhouse facility on the beach, south of the inlet. The new two-story-high Cabana Club, possibly designed by Schultze and Weaver, had ninety-seven cabanas stretching for three hundred yards in a semicircle facing the ocean. Each cabana contained a sun deck with awning, two dressing rooms and a shower. The new facility also included a large dining room and lounge, kitchens and staff rooms, a swimming pool, dressing rooms for members and guests without cabanas and two rooftop private "sun baths."

It became apparent that Mizner's original lounge should be enlarged and that the dance terrace between the lounge and the Cathedral Dining Room needed protection from cool ocean and lake breezes. Geist commissioned Marion Sims Wyeth, the architect of his Golf View Road house in Palm Beach, to design the additions. Wyeth, a graduate of both Princeton and the École des Beaux-Arts, came to Palm Beach in 1919 to see a house he had designed in the offices of Carrere & Hastings just before the beginning of World War I. While in the area, he received the commission for the first building of Good Samaritan Hospital in West Palm Beach and several small houses in Palm Beach and decided to open a Florida office. His restrained Spanish style of architecture and Ivy League background appealed to those who found Mizner and his architecture too flamboyant for their tastes. As the other society architect, he had designed the first Palm Beach house for E.F. Hutton and his wife, Marjorie Merriweather Post, across the street from the Geist house. When the Huttons decided to build Mar-a-Lago, Palm Beach's most famous mansion, Wyeth became their architect, only to have New York architect and set designer Joseph Urban brought in to complete the very ornate exterior decoration. Wyeth later said "It isn't my taste…I don't want anyone to think I was the architect in charge." The addition to the lounge extended out onto the lake, and numerous engineering drawings showed its steel piling support, though the architectural details of the extension matched Mizner's original design. Wyeth created a new cloister enclosing the dance terrace. Glazed double Gothic pointed arches in harmony with the lounge and dining room faced the lake, while seven wide, round arches supported by classical cast-stone columns faced the terrace. The cloister addition allowed the terrace to be used during warm winter nights for romantic starlit after-dinner entertainment.

When Geist purchased the Boca Raton property, he said he planned to carry on the projects of the Mizner Development Corporation. In June 1930, he began construction of two houses on Camino Real for investment purposes and with the hope of reviving the stagnant real estate market. Designed by Wyeth, the Spanish-style stucco houses with quarry keystone trim were two stories with four bedrooms. One had a patio enclosed on four sides; the other, a patio enclosed on three sides. Both had large living and dining

This aerial taken during the 1950s shows the Schultze and Weaver designed saltwater pool at lower right. *Photo by Jim Leo, Boca Raton Historical Society.*

Guests at the Boca Raton Hotel enjoy the saltwater pool in the 1950s. It featured beautiful tile, ironwork and colonnades in keeping with the Mediterranean style. *Boca Raton Historical Society.*

This aerial view shows the Cabana Club at left, south of the inlet, with the Boca Raton Club visible on the west side of Lake Boca Raton, circa mid-1950s. *Boca Raton Historical Society.*

The Cabana Club, built circa 1931, was the Boca Raton Club's beachside facility, located south of the inlet. *Boca Raton Historical Society.*

Geist's Golf View Road home in Palm Beach was designed by Marion Syms Wyeth, an architect he commissioned to design additions to the Boca Raton Club. *Photo courtesy Donald W. Curl.*

This aerial view of the club shows the Wyeth addition to the original Mizner lounge and new "cloister" adjacent to the Cathedral Dining Room, at right. *Boca Raton Historical Society.*

This photo is of one of two houses designed by Wyeth for Geist on Camino Real, across the street from the entrance to the Boca Raton Club. *Boca Raton Historical Society.*

rooms and staff quarters. A later *Palm Beach Times* article claimed each house cost $45,000. The same article said that the club and Spanish River Land Company had let a total of $350,000 in contracts for the two houses, the Cabana Club, the inlet project and clubhouse improvements. During the 1931 season, the western house sold to Frederick B. Rentschler, founder of United Aircraft Corporation and a club member. Geist never found a buyer for the eastern house, which, over the years, he leased to club members who wished to take a house for the season.

While his first venture in real estate development proved unsuccessful, in 1936 he tried again in the very desirable area between the ocean and Intracoastal Waterway that Mizner had called the Distrito de Boca Raton. Geist had financed a bridge across the waterway that linked the Cabana Club to the hotel, as well as the Distrito area. In 1936, he built two houses, and in 1937 and 1938, two more, all designed by Maurice Fatio, who had succeeded Addison Mizner as Palm Beach's most fashionable society architect. Born into a well-to-do banking family in Geneva, he trained for his profession at Zurich's Polytech and came to the United States in 1920. His very real talent, great personal charm and extremely good looks had furthered his success and given him clients like Harold S. Vanderbilt, his brother William K. Vanderbilt Jr., and their sister, Madame Louis Jacques Balsan, the former Duchess of Marlborough. Fatio chose the tropical Georgian style popular in Palm Beach in the 1930s for the Boca Raton houses.

This house on Cocoanut Road, in what Mizner had called the "Distrito" section, was one of four designed for Geist by Maurice Fatio in the late 1930s. *Boca Raton Historical Society.*

All were two stories with three or four bedrooms and quarters for two or three staff. Geist placed the houses in four different areas of the tract to encourage additional sales and construction. He did see three of the houses sell shortly after their construction, though they failed to restart the boom.

In 1938, Geist also commissioned Fatio to convert the little-used indoor club swimming pool into an auditorium. Since most club members came to Florida to spend time in the sun, an indoor pool had proved unpopular. On the other hand, from the first, movie nights proved very popular. While Geist installed a projector and screen in Mizner's lounge, it was never a satisfactory theatre. The new auditorium, with its extremely good acoustics, formal stage and large movie screen, became an immediate success.

Clarence Geist ran the Boca Raton Club for eight years, insisting that it remain completely private, with only members and their guests securing admission through its heavily guarded gates. One source said that almost none of the tourists driving down Federal Highway and seeing its towers had ever heard of the club. The Palm Beach clubs helped society reporters by giving them guest lists and allowing them to attend important events. The Boca Raton Club, under Geist, never gave out members' names or allowed publicity of its social activities. When a club event did make the society columns of the *New York Times* or the *Palm Beach Post*, the "item" usually came from someone mentioned in the article, not a club public relations officer.

1. This brochure cover for the Mizner Development Corporation's "Boca Raton" development features an image of the Cloister Inn, circa 1926. *Boca Raton Historical Society.*

2. A color postcard captures the beautiful Boca Raton Club from the air in the 1930s. *Boca Raton Historical Society.*

3. The statue of a slave girl and the surrounding fountain were designed by Italian artist Ettore Pellegatta for the Boca Raton Club in 1929. *Boca Raton Historical Society.*

4. Shortly after the Boca Raton Club's opening in 1930, owner Geist commissioned Marion Syms Wyeth to complete a second "cloister" for the hotel adjacent the Cathedral Dining Room. *Boca Raton Historical Society*.

5. Geist's improvements to Mizner's hotel included the completion of a beautiful Spanish-styled water garden in the original Cloister Inn courtyard. *Boca Raton Historical Society.*

6. The "grand staircase" in the east lobby of the Boca Raton Club was one of the most beautiful areas of the new hostelry. *Boca Raton Historical Society.*

7. Coffered ceilings and comfortable furnishings were characteristics of the new Boca Raton Club lobby in 1930. *Boca Raton Historical Society.*

8. The Cathedral Dining Room, a highlight of the Boca Raton Club, boasted coffered ceilings, gilt columns and an amazing view of Lake Boca Raton. *Boca Raton Historical Society.*

9. The "cloister" was one of the features of Mizner's Cloister Inn. Originally situated directly on the lakefront, a walkway and sea wall were added on the east side in the 1960s. *Boca Raton Historical Society*.

10. The Cloister Inn loggia has always provided an ideal setting for tea with its vista of the Cloister Garden. *Boca Raton Historical Society*.

11. This panoramic view reveals the main courtyard of today's Boca Raton Resort & Club, showing the Pellegatta statue and the main entrance at center. *Photo courtesy Peter Lorber.*

MAKE THIS WINTER VACATION THE MOST *Glorious of all* **STAY AT A SCHINE HOTEL**

The Boca Raton, Boca Raton, Fla.

The Roney Plaza, Miami Beach, Fla.

The Ambassador, Los Angeles, Calif.

The Gulf Stream, Miami Beach, Fla.

The McAllister, Miami, Fla.

Until you have lived at one of the magnificent Schine hotels in Southeastern Florida, or in Southern California, you will never know how wonderful these sun-filled lands can be for a winter vacation. For each of these hotels gives the beauty of its surroundings a finer and richer lustre, and adds its own great measure of gayety and excitement to the life of its locale...To enter one of them is to command every facility known to the art of gracious living—to enjoy matchless service and hospitality and to mingle with the world's distinguished travelers. To leave is to take with you the memory of an experience you will treasure as one of life's golden interludes. Yes, if you're going where the sun shines this winter, make *this* the most glorious vacation of all. Make your home a Schine Hotel—*the finest under the sun!*

SCHINE HOTELS *Finest under the Sun*

For Information and Reservations, Write: New York—445 Park Avenue, Murray Hill 8-0110
Chicago—333 N. Michigan Ave., Andover 3-6222
Los Angeles—3400 Wilshire Blvd., Dunkirk 9-6022

BOCA RATON HOTEL AND CLUB, Boca Raton, Fla. • THE RONEY PLAZA, Miami Beach, Fla. • THE GULF STREAM APARTMENTS AND COTTAGES, Miami Beach, Fla. • THE McALLISTER, Miami, Fla. • THE AMBASSADOR, Los Angeles, Calif. • THE RITZ-CARLTON, Atlantic City, N. J. • THE TEN EYCK, Albany, N. Y. THE HOTEL NORTHAMPTON AND WIGGINS OLD TAVERN, Northampton, Mass.

12. In 1944, hotelier J. Myer Schine acquired the Boca Raton Club. This advertisement, which appeared in *Holiday Magazine*, suggests that Schine was responsible for the hotel's famous pink color. *Boca Raton Historical Society.*

13. This postcard view shows the Boca Raton Club (now Hotel) from the as-yet-undeveloped Intracoastal Waterway looking north, circa 1950s. *Boca Raton Historical Society.*

14. The Schines and Davis spent millions refurbishing the hotel in the 1940s and '50s. This view shows the redecorated main lobby, circa 1957. *Boca Raton Historical Society.*

15. Constructed in the early 1930s, the Cabana Club was the hotel's beachfront establishment, located south of the inlet on A1A. *Boca Raton Historical Society.*

16. This image documents a guest room circa 1957, showing the vivid colors and "modern" furnishings favored at midcentury. *Boca Raton Historical Society.*

17. This brochure is a souvenir of the Arvida era of the Boca Raton Hotel. New management and changing economic times brought a focus on the convention market and less reliance on seasonal visitors. *Boca Raton Historical Society.*

18. Since the Mizner era, golf has been a major lure for guests at the hotel. This view shows the golf course on the west side of the hotel, circa late 1950s. *Boca Raton Historical Society.*

19. In 1969, Arvida completed the addition of a twenty-seven-story tower on the site of the southeast corner of Mizner's Cloister Inn, dramatically changing the hotel's skyline. *Photo by Jim Leo, Boca Raton Historical Society.*

20. The historic sections of the Boca Raton Resort & Club have stood the test of time, as shown in this 2007 photo of the main courtyard. *Photo by Michael Caldwell, courtesy LXR Luxury Resorts.*

21. This panoramic view reveals the Boca Raton Resort & Club, with its many additions and neighboring condominiums, looking west across Lake Boca Raton, circa 2008. *Photo courtesy Peter Lorber.*

The Schultze and Weaver additions for the Boca Raton Club included a large indoor saltwater pool, located in what is today the Valencia Room. *Boca Raton Historical Society.*

The indoor pool at the club proved unpopular, so in 1938 Geist commissioned Palm Beach architect Maurice Fatio to convert the room to an auditorium. *Boca Raton Historical Society.*

There were a few exceptions to the rule. In the mid-1930s, C.O. Smith, a reporter for the Southam chain of Canadian newspapers, visited the club and interviewed Geist, though in his article he revealed no members' names and did not describe the clubhouse. W.J. Southam, who owned the newspapers, belonged to the club as he owned one of the few oceanfront houses in Boca Raton. He probably provided the introduction for his reporter whose article lavished praise on both the club and its creator. He justified his lack of description of the club on the briefness of the article and his need to employ "adjectives that would seem sheer exaggeration," though he called it "palatial and amazingly beautiful." Geist said he created the club for the members to have "a winter home with more of the comforts and none of the responsibilities of a private house." He claimed success because "I never went into this to make money." Smith concluded that Geist's exceptional business ability, combined with his imagination, allowed him to conceive and construct such an "architectural gem."

In February 1937, the *New York Times* told of a dinner held at the club in honor of Mr. and Mrs. Owen D. Young, who had been married a few days before in St. Augustine. Young, the chairman of the General Electric Corporation, a well-known diplomat of the 1920s and author of the 1929 Young Plan for Germany, was a college classmate at St. Lawrence University of the host, Judge Charles W. Appleton, who served as vice president of General Electric. An earlier *Times* article described the wedding in the

The impressive new lobby of the Boca Raton Club extended the entire length of the northern section of the building. *Photo by Townsend, Boca Raton Historical Society.*

The east and west side of the main lobby of the Boca Raton Club featured beautifully painted coffered ceilings and luxurious appointments and plants. *Photo by Frank E. Geisler, Boca Raton Historical Society.*

The Cloister Garden was added circa 1929 to the central courtyard of Mizner's inn. It featured channeled waterways and fountains in the Spanish style. *Photo by Townsend, Boca Raton Historical Society.*

This view of the Cloister Garden is looking north toward Mizner's loggia and the Cloister Inn tower, at left. *Photo by Townsend, Boca Raton Historical Society.*

ancient city's Trinity Church. The dinner, for over forty guests, started with cocktails on the patio and continued in the great dining hall, where one large square table had elaborate decorations of orange blossoms and lighted white tapers. Guests included the bride and groom's married children and, among others, the B.C. Forbes, who founded *Forbes Magazine*; the Silas H. Strawns, a well-known Chicago attorney; Mrs. Edward Everett Gann, sister of Vice President Curtis; Mrs. Henry L. Doherty; the artist Alexander Calder; and Mr. and Mrs. Clarence H. Geist. It must be assumed that some of these guests were members of the club.

Theodore Pratt's magazine articles and booklet on Boca Raton are the source of many of the stories about Geist, the amazingly eccentric multimillionaire who ruled over his club like a Russian czar. Most show an extremely impolite man who enjoyed particularly boorish behavior. He included a story of Geist parading through the club lobby in his bathrobe, entering an already crowded elevator and ordering the attendant to take him to the sixth floor without stopping for the other passengers. Another claimed he held up the start of the movies until he arrived, often very late. His nephew suggests that all these tales are part of a mythology developed to make Geist seem more interesting to Pratt's readers. There are no other sources for the stories. One Pratt story claims that, in case he tired, Geist had his driver follow him on the golf course "straight down the fairway and up to the green." All evidence points to Geist's passionate love for golf. In the 1920s, he imported a professional golfer from Scotland to help him and his daughters improve their games. In Boca Raton, Tommy Armour, one of the best golfers of the 1920s and 1930s, served as his club's golf pro. Moreover, he spent millions of dollars to build and develop his golf courses into two of the best in the country. Would he risk the damage a car could do to his courses? Pratt also said that Geist had a great fear of being kidnapped and moved around the club surrounded by machine gun–carrying guards, changed rooms almost nightly and refused to have his photograph taken. Certainly, there were guards at the club gates, more to keep out uninvited guests than potential kidnapers. He had a suite of rooms on the sixth floor and there is no evidence that he changed from room to room. And he did pose for a number of photographs.

Clarence Geist died on June 12, 1938, at his Villanova estate. Earlier estimates had placed Geist's fortune at around $50 million. When lawyers filed the federal inheritance tax return in 1939, it claimed an estate valued at just over $54 million, with taxes owed to the United States and Pennsylvania governments of a little more than $30 million. He left the entire estate in trust to his widow and three daughters. Unfortunately, his property was liquidated during the Depression and after the New Deal–imposed inheritance tax. When executors finally settled the estate in March 1940, it had shrunk to $161,063, though this failed to take into account the several trusts. The Seaview Club, at first, seemed a casualty of his death when the Geist estate won a judgment against the club for over $500,000 and a judge ordered it sold. Its members came to the rescue, with each buying five $1,000 shares of stock in the club.

As for the Boca Raton Club, its owner had only stated the obvious when he told Southam's reporter he did not start the club to make money. An audit after Geist's death

Clarence Geist completed the dredging of the shallow Lake Boca Raton to make way for his boat-loving guests, shown gathered at the docks at the rear of the hotel in the 1930s. *Boca Raton Historical Society.*

This view from Lake Boca Raton, looking northwest, shows the original Cloister Inn, with the additional wings of the Boca Raton Club in the background, circa 1933. *Photo by Clifford Norton, Boca Raton Historical Society.*

discovered it had never turned a profit and that its owner had subsidized its operations from the beginning. This he continued, leaving a trust of $100,000 for each of the next five years. Florence Geist continued to run the club much as her husband had, as can be seen in a February 1941 article from the *Palm Beach Daily News* telling about Archduke Otto, pretender to the Austrian throne, staying at the "snorty" Boca Raton Club for its privacy. The author told about its famed security saying, "it's harder to gatecrash than Tuxedo Park" and that, upon entering, you "find a super-luxury hotel-like club done in heavy Spanish style where the lights are soft, the voices hushed, and an eminently correct sense of gloom pervades all." Florence Geist ran the club until 1942, when the Army Air Corps took over the clubhouse.

Chapter 3

The Boca Raton Hotel and Club

On May 15, 1942, Robert F. Lawrence, manager of the Boca Raton Club, said that he expected the vanguard of Army Air Corps officers and men to arrive any day to occupy the club and establish a "big new radio school." Some newspaper accounts said the corps "invaded" Boca Raton, while others told of the entire town being forced to join the United States Army. Actually, the Air Corps came at the invitation of town officials. After the attack on Pearl Harbor, Boca Raton's mayor, J.C. Mitchell, convinced the town council that an army base would be good for town development. He then traveled to Washington to persuade federal government officials. There he found mayors from the country over, bent on the same mission and all convinced they had a right to a military base. After being shuffled from one war department to another, Mitchell finally received a commitment that Boca Raton would be considered as a base site.

The Air Corps had decided to build a training base in southeast Florida, though Boca Raton had to compete with Vero Beach and Fort Pierce for the prize. In the competition, Boca Raton's advantage could once again be traced to the club. Early in 1935, club manager Gordon B. Anderson told town officials that many of the club's members now owned airplanes and thought Boca Raton should build an airport for their convenience. The town government agreed, and although it had no money to build an airport, it received title to "worthless land" west of town owned by Flagler's Model Land Company. Using the land and the promise to support an airport superintendent and to provide labor and equipment, the town applied for a WPA project in 1936. When the WPA questioned Boca Raton's commitments as insufficient, Anderson pressured the town to pledge a $15,000 donation of rock to pave the runways, equipment rentals and labor. When this still failed to budge the WPA, Anderson spent "a very profitable day in Washington," and work started on the airport before the end of 1936.

Unfortunately, before its completion, the money ran out, and Anderson, wishing to have the facility as soon as possible, convinced town officials to work with the club to finish the project. While completed in July, it still had to pass government inspection.

The "brass" inspects the temporary quarters of the Boca Raton Army Airfield at the Boca Raton Club, circa 1942. *Photo by the U.S. AAF Training Command, Skeele Collection, Boca Raton Historical Society.*

Anderson, fearful that an airport for the millionaires of the Boca Raton Club might have its approval delayed, told town officials to argue that many commercial and military airplanes flew across Palm Beach County each day with no landing field between Miami and West Palm Beach. In September 1929, an aerial photographer assigned to document the land owned by Clarence Geist crashed his plane trying to land on the club's south golf course. Anderson urged them to use this example to make their case. The cooperation between town and club worked, and when General Henry "Hap" Arnold led a group of officers to southeast Florida to choose a site for the new school, Boca Raton's airport gave it a decided advantage.

General Arnold searched for a site to train men in a new tracking technique called radar. In 1941, the Army Air Corps Technical School for Radar had been founded at Scott Field near Chicago, though the school had quickly outgrown the available space. Moreover, for radar training, shipping lanes providing "targets" were necessary. The heavy shipping traffic off the southeastern coast of Florida seemed perfect for the purpose, as did the many days of ideal flying weather. A further advantage came because an Army Signal Corps radar school had been established at Camp Murphy, just north of the Palm Beach County line, allowing the two schools to easily exchange information and personnel.

When General Arnold arrived in Boca Raton, a tropical storm had flooded town streets and left the airport standing in six inches of water, seemingly dashing all hope of it becoming the site of the new base. Nonetheless, Arnold saw that the high ground west of the airport remained dry, and realizing that the acreage existed to expand the small facility, he recommended Boca Raton for the training school.

Various branches of the armed forces had commandeered hotels from Miami Beach to Palm Beach, though few were as luxurious as the Boca Raton Club. Harold A. Turner, who later established a plant nursery and served as mayor of the town, directed the club's ground staff, which he later said had "dwindled to four or five." He and his staff, who thought "that Air Force personnel swarming all over the place would be catastrophic for the club," set up headquarters in the Administration Buildings and began to store the club's most valuable furnishings. Rare antiques, valuable paintings and tapestries and expensive Oriental rugs were placed in rooms that could be sealed. When possible, they also placed padded coverings over carved columns for protection. Turner said that before the small crew could finish, the first Air Force men arrived several days before expected and he had to abandon his conservation efforts. This resulted in rugs and carpets that were damaged beyond use "in a first class atmosphere such as the club." During the "army occupation," he tried to prevent as much damage as possible to the property. When the army moved in, it replaced the lavish furnishing with army cots placed four to a room for the men, though officers did receive private quarters. Sally J. Ling, in *Small Town, Big Secrets, Inside the Boca Raton Army Air Field During World War II*, tells of one aviation cadet who arrived at the club early and was set to work removing carpeting and cleaning the cement floors "with GI soap and razor blades" to make it shine. The air force men used all the facilities of the club for both training and recreation, including the swimming pools, tennis courts, Cabana Club and even the golf courses where Turner claimed they dug fox holes.

The Air Corps meant to occupy the club only until it constructed the base west of town. Drollene P. Brown, in her article "World War II in Boca Raton: The Home Front" in the *Spanish River Papers*, said that by May 1942, land for the base had been acquired, and "with wartime speed, the engineers set to work." In June, Colonel Arnold MacSpadden came to Boca Raton to supervise construction of the base designed in a "dispersed layout" because of possible bombings along the Florida east coast. Brown said he used fourteen contractors, thirty-five hundred construction workers and $12 million to finish the first phase of the project. The base opened for its first training class in October, and by January 1943, three five-thousand-foot-long runways and over eight hundred structures were ready to receive the airmen. As the Army Air Corps' only radar training school during World War II, the Boca Raton base had trained thousands of troops by the war's end.

With housing available on the base, most airmen left the club, though a number of officers remained. A *New York Times* article on June 20, 1943, said that the army planned to surrender the lease of the Boca Raton Club to the C.H. Geist Trust in September 1943 as part of a plan to return 206 hotels in New Jersey, Illinois, Michigan and Florida to their owners. The army said it could do this because of the movement of so many air units overseas. The Air Corps still controlled the club in October 1944, when a hurricane threatened southeastern Florida. Ling said that, on October 17, base officers rushed several hundred airmen to the club to make preparations for a general evacuation of both the field personnel and their civilian wives and children. Although crowded into an

To ensure the safety of the luxurious interiors, the hotel furnishings were packed away for the duration of the war, as shown in this wartime photo of the Cathedral Dining Room. *Photo by the U.S. AAF Training Command, Skeele Collection, Boca Raton Historical Society.*

During the Air Corps' takeover of the Boca Raton Club, antiques were packed away and the elaborate columns were wrapped for protection. Here, furnishings are readied for storage in the lobby. *Photo by the U.S. AAF Training Command, Skeele Collection, Boca Raton Historical Society.*

The Boca Raton Club was one of the most luxurious "barracks" of World War II. Servicemen could get in a little R&R on the golf course of the hotel. *Photo by the U.S. AAF Training Command, Boca Raton Historical Society.*

The hotel became temporary training grounds, as well as barracks. In this photo, servicemen complete water training at the Boca Raton Club's pool, circa 1943. *Photo by the U.S. AAF Training Command, Skeele Collection, Boca Raton Historical Society.*

Colonel Lawrence J. Carr, commanding officer; Colonel Thomas L. Bryan; and Lieutenant Colonel Charles W. Skeele meet in Carr's office at the Boca Raton Club, circa 1942. *Photo by the U.S. AAF Training Command, Skeele Collection, Boca Raton Historical Society.*

inadequate space, all survived the hurricane and the airmen returned to base training three days later. The army returned the club to civilian control in December 1944, and the remaining officers moved to the base. Until then, the Boca Raton Club and the Cabana Club had served officers for their recreational needs. Ling said the Army Air Corps now built a new officers' club on the base, which opened with many festivities on July 4, 1945.

In March 1944, James Carroll, manager of the Roney Plaza Hotel in Miami Beach, announced that his employer, J. Myer Schine, had purchased the Boca Raton Club for $3 million. He added that the price included the "whole village" with its city hall, fire department, service buildings, two golf courses, hundreds of acres of land and a number of houses. On the following day, a *Palm Beach Post* article entitled "You Can't Just Buy a Village!" detailed Boca Raton citizens' reaction to Carroll's claim. The reporter said that many good burghers, confused by the wild rumor that a "moneyed gentleman from Miami" bought them "lock stock and barrel" has caused "puckers of bewilderment to cloud their faces." In fact, Police Chief William H. Brown declared that the owner of the Roney Plaza never purchased the town. "A person can't walk in, peel off a roll of bills, and buy a town." Brown pointed out that Schine purchased only the interests of the Clarence H. Geist estate of the clubhouse, golf courses and around three hundred acres of land. Robert F. Lawrence, manager of the Boca Raton Club, agreed with him and said he also owned property in the town. Nonetheless, the reporter asserted that the citizens of Boca Raton "are clinging grimly to their front porches, armed only with righteous indignation but pledged to battle this monstrous resurgence of free-bootery."

In a 1976 interview for the Boca Raton Historical Society, Schine's wife, Hildegarde Feldman Schine, remembered traveling up to Boca Raton from her home in the Roney Plaza after New York jeweler Harry Winston told her the club might be available. Her husband, who was in New York, gave her a check to complete the purchase if she approved. When she arrived, she found the place "plastered" with soldiers who had "Maywood-Wakefield [*sic*] beds and little bureaus." After viewing the furniture, the bare public rooms and the columns covered by plywood she told the caretaker showing her around that this "is a really ugly place." He said no and took a piece of plywood off to show her the wonderful columns underneath, and she immediately made the purchase.

J. Myer Schine, born in Latvia in 1892 and brought to the United States as a child by his parents, grew up in Gloversville, New York, a small city to the north and west of Albany. His 1971 *New York Times* obituary said he started as a candy butcher boy and dress salesman and, with his savings, purchased a roller rink in Gloversville and invested the profits in other properties. His brother Louis's 1956 *New York Times* obituary said that they invested $1,500 in savings in the Gloversville Hippodrome nickelodeon and "from this modest beginning the two brothers were to become millionaires." The Hippodrome became the first in a chain of over one hundred theatres in New York, Ohio, Kentucky, Maryland and Delaware owned by the brothers. When they purchased the Boca Raton Club, the brothers also owned, among other properties, the Ambassador Hotel in Los Angeles; the Roney Plaza and Gulf Stream Hotels in Miami Beach; the McAllister in Miami; the Northampton in Northampton, Massachusetts; the Queensbury in Glen Falls, New York; the Ten Eyck in Albany; and the Atlantic City Ritz-Carlton.

Before the Air Corps turned the club over to the Schine interests, it hired Palm Beach architect John L. Volk to restore the building to its prewar condition. The Schines then started a modernization program before they opened the club as a hotel. They retained Walter P. Margulies, an industrial designer, as a consultant and embarked on a $4.1 million project that included several of their hotels. Hildegarde Schine said Christopher Caston, a German designer and friend of the Geists, took charge of the Boca Raton hotel. When she and her husband decided to move to Boca Raton from the Roney Plaza, they had Don Loper, a California decorator, redo the old Geist suite on the sixth floor. Overall, Mrs. Schine said they spent $1 million in refurbishing the hotel and Cabana Club.

The major architectural change of this period created a large new dining room from the old dance patio. Called the Patio Royale, its entry from the club lobby was through the Mizner dining room, now cut in two with a large meeting room formed from its upper half and named the Mizner room. The roof over the Patio Royale dance floor retracted, allowing romantic starlit evenings to continue. The Mizner loggia also received a glass wall overlooking the courtyard. In general, the decorators' work meant changing the dark wood of the furnishings of the earlier era into the lighter midcentury modern pieces so popular after the war. Although the architecture remained little changed, the new hotel took on a bland institutional look that seemed more at home in postwar Miami Beach than Boca Raton.

Third owner of the Boca Raton Hotel J. Myer Schine and his wife, Hildegard, are shown in this 1968 portrait. They were active members of the local community. *Photo by Jim Leo, Boca Raton Historical Society.*

During the Schine era, Mizner's original dining room, later a lounge, was divided horizontally. The top floor became the Mizner Room, a popular meeting space. *Boca Raton Historical Society.*

The Schines commissioned a retractable awning over the area called the Patio Royale, just outside the Cathedral Dining Room. Guests could enjoy performances like the one shown here, circa 1950. *Boca Raton Historical Society.*

The guest rooms were particularly "updated" by the Schines. Old-world styles were replaced with popular 1950s features, like the bold wallpaper and sleek furniture shown here. *Boca Raton Historical Society.*

Refurbishing still continued as the new Boca Raton Hotel and Club opened on January 15, 1945. When *Holiday* magazine visited the "giant white pile of a hotel" six years later, it found that opening it to the public had failed to tarnish the resort's "atmosphere of 14-karat glitter." According to the magazine, everything "at Boca is approximately twice life-sized, including the cakes of soap, the match folders, and the total on the bills." Its "impeccable" style of operation, which included one employee for each guest, still drew the leaders of American life and international society. Vice President Alben Barkley spent part of his honeymoon at the hotel, whose other recent guests included former President Hoover, the Duke and Duchess of Windsor, Irving Berlin, Danny Kaye, Governor Harold Stassen, Hollywood gossip columnist Louella Parsons and the New York Central's Robert R. Young. The magazine also noted that a "comfortable" corner suite for two went for eighty-five dollars a night and a cabana for seventy-five dollars a week. Golf remained the major attraction, and Tommy Armour from the club days was still the professional.

One continuing question about the Boca Raton Hotel and Club concerns its exterior color. The most often heard answer claims that Mizner used his favorite pink paint, establishing its color tradition. Unfortunately, Mizner never favored the color pink and rarely used it for his Palm Beach buildings. When he specified pink for the Everglades residential villas, he called for "soft Mediterranean colors," with only one of the seven villas actually painted pink. Another villa was painted white, which meant that Mizner considered it a Mediterranean color. Moreover, when he used pink, it was usually extremely soft and pastel, like a Brooks Brothers shirt. There are no color photographs of the Cloister Inn. In black-and-white photographs, the stone entrance pavilion appears natural and unpainted; the rest of the build seems extremely light and could be white. We know from many descriptions that the lobby walls were white. The *Holiday* article both called it the "giant white pile of a hotel" and used a color photograph showing the white upper sections of the Schultze and Weaver club building. One Boca Raton tradition has long held that the hotel acquired its deep dusty rose color during the Schine era. This tradition also claims that Hildegarde Schine favored this color. Some evidence for this can be found in the same issue of *Holiday*. An advertisement for the Schine Hotel Corporation pictures small drawings of its Florida hotels, including the one in Boca Raton. All are shown in deep dusty rose.

When the Schines moved to Boca Raton in 1948, Hildegarde Schine immediately became involved in the life of the community. She had first attempted to establish friendly relations with the town's people shortly after buying the hotel. On hearing that few of them had ever "set foot" in the club, she "gave a party" and invited everyone. At the party, she told them the club was becoming a public hotel and they could use all its facilities, as long as they rented a cabana and paid for their meals. As she still found the town's people "suspicious," and since she was "the type of person who wanted to get involved and do things," she joined a group of women who had established a library in

Under J. Myer Schine's management, the Boca Raton Club became the Boca Raton Hotel and Club. This Schine-era advertisement lures visitors to "Florida's Secret Paradise." *Boca Raton Historical Society.*

Here, the Duke of Windsor, a frequent hotel visitor in the 1950s, poses with tennis pro Fred Perry and golf pro Tommy Armour. *Photo by National Resort Photographers, Boca Raton Historical Society.*

Local beauty Dorothy Steiner, "Miss Florida 1957," poses on the diving board of the Cabana Club pool in the late 1950s. *Photo by Margaret Olsson, Boca Raton Historical Society.*

town hall. When the town needed the space and the women realized it was inadequate for a library, they decided to raise money for their own building. Hildegarde Schine said she found many of the women painted or did craft work, so she organized a show of their arts and crafts to raise funds for a new library. This led to the formation of the Art Guild. The women held musicals, gave card parties and teas and sponsored art exhibits. When they had raised $85,000, Schine gave his wife a downtown lot for the two organizations. She found the lot too small to meet city ordinance parking requirements and sold it for $50,000, which she divided between the two organizations. The library found a home on Second Avenue and the Art Guild in Floresta.

Hildegarde Schine and Lavonne Mouw, the wife of a local contractor, also sponsored musicals to raise money for the Methodist Church. Mrs. Schine, born in Gloversville, New York, graduated from Syracuse University with a fine and liberal arts degree and played both the piano and organ all her life. She said that one day the "very good looking minister" said that when he came to Boca Raton he had to rent chairs from a funeral home for services, the choir had no robes, there was no organ or piano and no books. "Thanks to Mrs. Schine and Mrs. Mouw we have all these things. We also have money in the bank." According to Hildegarde Schine, Mrs. Mouw turned to her and said, "I guess we fixed up your church." She answered, "I'm not Methodist, I'm Jewish! You're a Methodist aren't you?" Mrs. Mouw answered, "No, I'm Presbyterian."

Although the names of its members are unknown in most cases, it has always been assumed that the Boca Raton Club never accepted Jewish members. This was certainly true of Clarence Geist's Palm Beach clubs and was accepted by most in Palm Beach society during this period. Rumor has always stated that the Schines continued the policy of excluding Jews. This is certainly untrue. In the Boca Raton Hotel and Club magazine, *The Guest Book*, for February 15, 1947, four out of eight photographs picture Jewish guests, including the young daughter of the Gerald Bronfman family of Montreal.

Hildegarde Schine also claimed that she arranged for the filming of Theodore Pratt's best-known novel, *The Barefoot Mailman*. When Irving Thalberg and Sylvan Simon, producers with Columbia Pictures, visited the Schines at the hotel, she told them how much she enjoyed the book. They read it and offered Pratt a contract that same weekend.

The Schines received national attention in 1954 through their son, G. David Schine. The younger Schine had briefly served as president of the Schine Hotel Corporation before his father reclaimed the title. He then acted as an unpaid consultant to Senator Joseph R. McCarthy's communist-hunting Senate Permanent Investigations subcommittee. Schine had accompanied Roy M. Cohn, a committee counsel, on investigative trips until he was drafted into the army as a private. The secretary of the army, Robert T. Stevens, claimed that Cohn and McCarthy exerted undue influence to gain Schine a commission. They, in turn, charged Stevens with "blackmail" by trying to stop their investigations of communist subversion at Fort Monmouth in New Jersey. The dispute lead to one of the earliest televised senate hearings in the spring of 1954, which ended with McCarthy's censure by his Senate colleagues. G. David Schine also caused controversy within the Schine companies, quarreling with the managers of the Roney Plaza Hotel and losing money on several ventures, including a carpeted indoor ski slope that operated on a conveyor belt. He married a former Miss Universe from Sweden, and after serving as manager of the Ambassador Hotel, he entered the movie business, acting as executive producer of the *French Connection*. He, his wife and his pilot son died in a crash of their small plane in California in June 1996.

The 1947 hurricane caused flooding in many areas of Boca Raton, severely damaged many of the "temporary" structures on the Air Field and destroyed the cabanas at the Cabana Club. Schine both rebuilt the cabanas and added many more to the structure. The storm had also washed away the beach up to the entrance to the dining room. Schine had a new groin built at the south end of the property, which saved the Cabana Club beach. Unfortunately, it also caused further erosion from the Cabana Club south to Deerfield Beach.

Schine, like Clarence Geist, also attempted to start development of Mizner's Distrito, now known as "the Estates." He hired Norman Bel Geddes, an industrial designer, to plan seven houses for the subdivision. Since Bel Geddes was unregistered as an architect, the Delray Beach firm of Robert Blake and Henry Pope signed the drawings. Again, like the Geist scheme, Schine located the new houses on several different streets. The time was right, and these houses, and many more lots, sold.

In 1955, Schine started construction of Boca Raton's first shopping center in the city's downtown area. F. Byron Parks, director of real estate for the hotel, said it took him three years to put together the nineteen acres of twenty-five-foot lots Mizner had sold in the

The hurricane of September 1947 caused extensive damage to the "temporary" structures of the army Air Field and destroyed the cabanas at the Cabana Club. *Boca Raton Historical Society.*

1920s. Planned as a large retail complex with one thousand parking spaces, Gamble, Pownall and Gilroy, Fort Lauderdale architects, designed a Kwik-Check supermarket, a forerunner of Winn-Dixie and a Love's Drug Store to inaugurate the project. Parks said it was only one of a series of projects planned "to make Boca Raton the most beautiful resort spot on the Gold Coast." The center, known to several generations of Boca Raton residents as the "Pink Plaza," is today Royal Palm Place and the location of the Addison Mizner statue.

In 1956, the Schines sold the Boca Raton Hotel and Club to Arthur Vining Davis for $22.5 million in one of the largest real estate transactions in Florida history. Hildegarde Schine later claimed they sold because J. Myer's brother, Louis Schine, who owned a third of the hotel, was dying of cancer. While this may be true, the close to $20 million profit certainly played a role. Although Davis purchased all the properties associated with the hotel and club, including all oceanfront land south of Palmetto Park Road, Schine retained title to the oceanfront land he had purchased in north Boca Raton. The Schines also remained in the city, buying property fronting the Intracoastal Waterway at 1281 Spanish River Road in the Estates section. J. Myer Schine developed the Sun and Surf Club subdivision on some of his remaining property, and Hildegarde Schine remained active in Boca Raton community affairs.

In September 1965, J. Myer Schine set off several legal battles when he attempted to sell the remaining twelve hotels, sixty theatres, and three thousand acres of mostly beachfront land in Palm Beach and Boca Raton to Realty Equities Corporation of

New York for $75 million. The real estate partnership of attorney Lawrence A. Wien and Harry B. Helmsley, who owned a 114-year lease on the Empire State Building and coast-to-coast property holdings valued at close to $900 million, claimed that Schine had agreed in July 1965 to sell them the same properties for $64 million. A *New York Times* article of September 3, 1965, said that Schine failed to follow through on the deal because of Wein and Helmsley's unilateral announcement of the sale and because he believed they treated him like an old man, desperate to dispose of his properties. Legal maneuvering, charges and countercharges followed until all parties agreed to hearings before the American Arbitration Association, which ruled in favor of the Realty Equities deal. Then, in 1967, Reality Equities Corporation tried to back out of its agreement because of Schine's inability to perform on the bulk of the agreement and deliver clear title for the Ambassador Hotel. Schine claimed that the property was marketable, and once again the parties entered arbitration, which was decided in Schine's favor.

J. Myer Schine died on May 8, 1971, in New York City, where the Schines maintained an apartment at Fifth Avenue and Sixty-sixth Street. Hildegard Schine continued to spend winters in her Intracoastal Waterway residence and maintained her many local interests. During the 1960s and 1970s, first she and her husband and then she alone sold their beachfront property to the City of Boca Raton. This land comprised much of

This rustic structure was home to the hotel's "fleet" of two yachts until the late 1950s. It stood on the east side of the Intracoastal, just south of the Camino Real bridge. *Photo by Jim Leo, Boca Raton Historical Society.*

Spanish River Park and all sixty-seven acres of what became Red Reef Park. Al Alford, mayor at the time of the Red Reef Park negotiations, said, "Our beaches are our most wonderful natural asset, and we owe the Schines a debt of gratitude for not piecemealing it out. We'd be a totally different community otherwise." Hildegarde Schine died at her summer home in the Catskills on September 7, 1994, just days before her planned return to Boca Raton for the winter.

Chapter 4

Arthur Vining Davis and the Arvida Years

When Arthur Vining Davis purchased the Boca Raton Hotel and Club on February 22, 1956, he was only months away from his ninetieth birthday. While most people nearing ninety had retired years before, he still served as chairman of the Aluminum Corporation of America and had just started a new career as a major Florida developer. Davis, born in Sharon, Massachusetts, on March 30, 1867, was the son of the Reverend Perley Davis, a Congregational clergyman. He graduated at the top of his class from Amherst College in 1888 and immediately accepted a job in Pittsburgh with Charles Martin Hall, who had discovered a new process for the production of aluminum. Hall's firm, originally known as the Pittsburgh-Reduction Company, received financial backing from the Mellon family. It became the Aluminum Corporation of America, or Alcoa, in 1908, and Davis became its president two years later. In 1928, Davis became Alcoa's chairman, a position he held for almost forty years.

The market for the new metal grew steadily, as did the company. In particular, the aviation industry and America's large Air Force during World War II produced a huge new demand for aluminum for airplanes. In the 1930s, the Justice Department filed an antitrust suit against Aluminum Corporation of America, charging that seven people—including three members of the Mellon family, Davis, the trustees of the Duke Endowment and Doris Duke—owned almost 60 percent of Alcoa and over 60 percent of Aluminium Limited, or Alcan, a Canadian corporation formed to receive the stock of some thirty-six foreign corporations owned by Alcoa. Edward K. Davis, Arthur Vining Davis's brother, served as president of the Canadian company. Final judgment in the suit came fourteen years later in 1951. Under its terms, those who held stock in both corporations had to sell their Canadian holdings in the next ten years. As the Mellon shares in the Canadian company had been dispersed to children and trusts by 1951, Davis remained the largest single shareholder. While perhaps Davis had various reasons for his large Florida and Bahamian land purchases, his sale of the Canadian stock gave him the resources for the new investments.

This aerial view shows the full beauty of the Boca Raton Hotel and Club, looking west from across Lake Boca Raton, circa 1960. *Photo by Jim Leo, Boca Raton Historical Society.*

Davis, described by *Look* magazine as "a short, peppery, hawknosed, sharpeyed whitehaired publicity-hating man," began his massive land purchases when he moved his headquarters to Miami in 1948. By the time he bought the Boca Raton Hotel, he owned thousands of acres of land in Dade, Broward and Palm Beach Counties, property near St. Augustine and Tallahassee, over twenty thousand acres on Eleuthera in the Bahamas, where he built a resort, and many acres on Cuba's Isle of Pines, which he lost after Castro came to power. His diversified properties included, among others, an ice-cream plant, vegetable farms, a cement plant, a road-building concern, a steel-fabricating factory, a furniture plant and an airline.

In association with Stuart L. Moore, a hotel man and former vice president of the Southern division of Schine Hotels, Davis purchased six small inns in Delray Beach. He then bought the Boca Raton Hotel and Club and created Boca Raton Properties to manage them. Moore and Davis planned to allow guests of the Delray Beach properties to have full use of the Boca Raton facilities, making it "a huge country club." They also planned to develop their eleven hundred acres of land in Boca Raton with residences "of the right class." Claiming his basic ideas for Boca Raton stemmed from his love of architecture, Davis said:

This aerial view, looking north, shows the Camino Real fountain and Boca Raton Hotel as development of the area began in the late 1950s. *Photo by Jim Leo, Boca Raton Historical Society.*

In the accelerated pace of Florida's industrial and population growth, it seems to me important to preserve some sections of the state in the atmosphere of quiet luxury which once provided the motive for migration here. While Florida will always offer ideal home sites for the middle-income group which constitutes the bulk of the population, our increased national prosperity dictates that we provide also for the group whose accomplishments enable them to enjoy the finest. It is in this light that we plan to develop the Boca Raton area on a level second to none in the world.

Davis planned, like all of the previous owners of the hotel, to develop the city in the Mizner tradition.

Moore, who became president of Boca Raton Properties, began the new era by lengthening the hotel tourist season from Christmas to Easter and adding some "select" conventions after its close. He also hired "master decorator" Lawrence Colwell to spruce up the Cathedral Dining Room and complete the new Polo Lounge. To provide the "dramatic luster" necessary for the magnificent dining room, Colwell chose to finish all seventy-five of its columns in gold leaf. It took Bill Lowry of Delray Signs six weeks to apply the over five thousand square feet of imported leaf. Colwell then contrasted the

Decorator Lawrence Colwell improved the dramatic luster of the Cathedral Dining Room by applying five thousand square feet of gold leaf to its columns. *Photo by Jim Leo, Boca Raton Historical Society.*

brilliance of the gold with the deep tone of a royal purple carpet and specially designed and woven draperies. Colwell also designed gold and silver wall plaques featuring the B-R monogram capped by brightly colored banners, huge sculptured medallions in gold for the upper walls and outlined the richly ornamented vaulted ceiling in gold. Lowry painted a dado at the base of the walls in a faux marble design "in the modern manner" to lend contrast to the opulence of the columns and carpeting. For the Polo Lounge, Colwell designed and Lowry painted sixteen black-and-gold-framed murals of polo games in action from "the Eighteenth Century until now." Further decorating the room were replicas of famous polo trophies, and caps, shirts, mallets and saddles used by polo players. A large map showed the locations of polo clubs throughout North America. The Polo Lounge recognized that Davis, a fan of high-goal polo, had built a field and grandstands south of the hotel that became nationally renowned and a focal point for Palm Beach society.

To start the development of the city for the class of people Davis desired, he turned to Milton N. Weir and his Pompano Beach real estate company, appointing him as sales agent for his Boca Raton properties in May 1957. Weir formerly served as vice president

Boca Raton Hotel owner Arthur Vining Davis and his secretary, Evelyn Mitchell (at center), are joined by the Oak Brook (Illinois) Polo Team on the polo grounds, built just south of Camino Real, in 1958. *Photo by Jim Leo, Boca Raton Historical Society.*

in charge of New York real estate for the Gulf Oil Corporation. The Mellon family owned a major stake in Gulf Oil.

In August, now completely committed to his Florida ventures, Davis resigned as chairman of Alcoa. At the time, he said the pressures of his Florida business interests had prevented him from devoting the time and attention to Alcoa that he deemed "desirable and necessary." What he had devoted his time to became evident in September of the next year, when Davis placed most of his extensive real estate holdings into a new operating company. Known as Arvida Corporation, an acronym of Davis's name, the company hoped to raise as much as $35 million through a public offering of common stock. A group of investment banking concerns, headed by Carl M. Loeb, Rhoades and Company and Dominick and Dominick, planned to offer the new stock at around ten dollars a share after filing a registration statement with the Securities and Exchange Commission.

The new company held sixty-five hundred acres in Delray Beach and Boca Raton in Palm Beach County, including around seventy-five hundred feet of ocean frontage. It also included the Boca Raton Hotel and Club and other operating properties. It owned twenty-three thousand acres of land in Broward County west of Fort Lauderdale and Hollywood, and seventy-two thousand acres in Dade County, the largest block of privately owned land in the county. Davis, who retained over half of the stock in the new company, named himself chairman; Milton Weir Sr., president; and Milton Weir Jr., vice president and general manager. The same *New York Times* article that reported the formation of Arvida mentioned that Davis remained the largest single stockholder in Alcoa, with more than 900,000 shares out of 20,645,000. At the time, reports estimated his net worth as between $350 million and $500 million. Davis refused to comment on his wealth and gave few newspaper interviews. According to a widely told story, he made one exception. At a Miami party he overheard two men speculating on whether he was the second or third richest man in America. "Fifth," he said, and walked quickly away.

Davis had used the Arvida acronym before. When Alcoa constructed its first aluminum smelter on the Saguenay River, about 125 miles north of Quebec City in near wilderness, its model company town, designed for a population of fourteen thousand, was named Arvida. Under Davis's leadership, Alcoa built a town of detached houses on generous lots to sell to its employees at moderate prices and low interest. The company also provided all community services, including police and fire protection, schools and churches and shops. Arvida became a famous example of a model town and many considered it to be Davis's outstanding social achievement.

With the formation of Arvida Corporation, Davis once more found himself in trouble with a federal agency. The Securities and Exchange Commission charged on October 1, 1958, that publicity on the founding of the company and its plan to sell stock through its underwriter companies actually constituted a public offering, an attempt to sell the stock before registering it with the commission. The commission then asked the federal district court in New York for an injunction halting Arvida stock sales. A federal judge denied the injunction of October 18, saying that a press release could be considered a legitimate news item of general financial interest and "did not constitute an offer to sell."

Milton Weir considered the first land tract selected by Arvida for development to be the "jewel" of its vast holdings. The 450 acres directly south of the hotel had natural boundaries of the Intracoastal Waterway on the east, the Hillsboro River on the south, Federal Highway on the west and the hotel and golf course on the north. Work on the development, known as the Royal Palm Yacht and Country Club, started early in 1959. The tract contained the polo field and a nine-hole golf course that hotel pro Sam Snead often used to give lessons. Davis moved the polo field in 1960 to land on Glades Road, west of the Seaboard Railroad tracks. To prove the claim that Boca Raton was "the winter capital of polo," Davis invested $500,000 in the 89-acre site, creating two "emerald green grass playing fields," exercise and practice fields, stables for 146 ponies, locker rooms for players and living quarters for trainers, grooms and exercise boys. Golf architect Robert Trent Jones created a new eighteen-hole course for Royal Palm to maximize its exposure to as many of the subdivision's 742 lots as possible. Many additional lots fronted on the Intracoastal Waterway, the Hillsboro River or deep-water canals with direct access to the waterway. The price of lots started at $11,500 and went up to $40,000 for a waterway location. If the buyer agreed to start construction within six months of purchase, he received a 20 percent discount. By November 1959, Arvida had sold 220 lots valued

Guests of the Boca Raton Hotel pose with what looks to be a record marlin at the docks on the east side of Lake Boca Raton opposite the hotel, 1950s. *Photo by Margaret Olsson, Boca Raton Historical Society.*

at $3.75 million. The first house was completed on Silver Palm Road in January 1960. Local architect Howard E. McCall, Palm Beach architects Howard Chilton and John L. Volk and Fort Lauderdale architect Arthur H. Rude designed other early houses. The $5.5 million development costs included $1.25 million for placing the electrical utility system underground. Royal Palm also became Boca Raton's first gated community, with guarded entrances on the circle in front of the hotel and on South Federal Highway.

At the same time, Arvida organized the club at Royal Palm Yacht and Country Club with the ownership of a lot or house in Royal Palm a requirement for membership. Arvida owned the club and charged only $100 for membership. When club membership reached five hundred, the ownership was to pass to the members. Architect Robert Fitch Smith of Miami designed both the yacht and golf clubhouses in "Bahama-Colonial" style, with the first on a generously sized yacht basin with direct access to the waterway. Members acquired title to the club on January 1, 1964. In line with Davis's wishes, Royal Palm has remained one of Boca Raton's "best addresses" over the years.

Arvida also started to develop the University Park subdivision in 1959. Located north of Glades Road and just west of the Boca Raton city limits, its planned ten thousand lots were designed for middle-income families. In the same year, Arvida signed a contract with the Gulf Oil Corporation to construct and operate a chain of gasoline service stations and marine outlets throughout Florida. Arvida located one of its first Gulf gasoline stations on its property at Camino Real and Dixie Highway. In its first year, Arvida also purchased the John Ringling properties in Sarasota County for $13.5 million and planned to develop the tract with houses and hotels. In an August 1959 speech to the New York Society of Security Analysts, Weir reported that in its first year, Arvida had earned $3.5 million on about $16.6 million gross sales.

In February 1961, both Weirs resigned from Arvida, claiming they needed more time to devote to their family's real estate and banking interests. The year before Weir Sr. had founded the Boca Raton National Bank and served as its chairman. Moreover, although Arvida had a good first year, by 1961 it had lost $1.2 million on revenues of $6.1 million. In fact, the company continued in the red for the next two years. Davis felt he needed new blood in the president's chair. As president of Arvida, Weir had set the company on its course of careful, responsible development. As one writer said, he "continued the proud traditions of Addison Mizner." His Royal Palm Yacht and Country Club set the standard for residential development in the city and has become one of South Florida's most exclusive residential areas. Under his leadership, Arvida also negotiated and then paid $400,000 for a Boca Raton interchange on the Sunshine State Parkway, now the Florida Turnpike. When the state constructed the expressway, it considered Boca Raton too small to warrant an exit. Weir and his family also moved to Boca Raton and became active in community affairs, including support for the founding of the community hospital.

The Jacksonville real estate firm Stockton, Whatley, Davin and Company entered into a management contract with Arvida in 1961, and Brown L. Whatley, active in Florida real estate since the 1920s, took over as president. In the early 1960s, Whatley had seen the successful development of condominiums in Puerto Rico. As president of Arvida, he lobbied for the law that allowed the addition of condominium mortgage insurance to the

ROYAL PALM
YACHT &
COUNTRY CLUB
SECTION

MONDAY, APRIL 11, 1960

FORT LAUDERDALE NEWS

LUXURY COMMUNITY IN BOCA RATON NOW COMPLETE!

YACHT CLUB AND GOLF COURSE NOW OFFICIALLY OPEN AT ROYAL PALM YACHT & COUNTRY CLUB

Less than one year after development began, Arvida Realty Co. has transformed 450 acres immediately south and adjoining the internationally famous Boca Raton Hotel and Club into a magnificent residential community.

Enhanced by a rare and desirable setting, Royal Palm Yacht & Country Club boasts its own half-million-dollar Yacht Club, Golf Club, 18-hole championship golf course, and 743 homesites, many on winding waterways and bordering the

golf course. To date 459 homesites have been sold and 62 homes are under construction.

All utilities at Royal Palm have been placed underground. There are no poles or utility wires to mar the vistas of beautiful homes, placid waterways, and acres of fairways.

Rare is the setting. Magnificent are the facilities offered in Royal Palm Yacht & Country Club residential community, the most desirable on all of Florida's Gold Coast.

THE ROYAL PALM YACHT CLUB

The elegant Yacht Club looks out over broad fairways, meandering Hillsboro River and the Royal Palm marina. Its dining room will accommodate up to 500 dinner guests. Built at a cost in excess of $500,000, it is the social gathering place of the community.

THE ROYAL PALM GOLF AND COUNTRY CLUB

Golfers have their own club in Royal Palm. The dining room overlooks the broad 18th green, and the "19th Hole" features a Scottish Linksland mural in a setting of walnut paneling and plush custom-made carpeting. Sam Snead and his staff operate the pro shop and tutor Club members.

Arvida's Royal Palm Yacht and Country Club, developed just south of the hotel, became one of Boca Raton's "best addresses." *Boca Raton Historical Society.*

The grounds crew poses outside the west façade of the old pool, circa 1962. (Notice one of them is a woman.) *Photo by Jim Leo, Boca Raton Historical Society.*

National Housing Act, which set off the Florida condominium boom. Like Weir, Whatley also practiced restraint in developing Arvida's land, keeping Boca Raton's growth at a sensible pace. One writer said that Whatley believed that Arvida's attitude "is not wholly altruistic. Good planning is always the most profitable planning." Davis's death, just a year after Whatley became president, gave him the freedom to set Arvida's course with little interference for the next four years.

Arthur Vining Davis died on November 17, 1962, at the age of ninety-five at his Coral Gables estate, Journey's End. Although he had a heart attack in 1956 and fainted in a barber's chair in 1959, overall he remained in good health until just several days before his death, which set in motion many changes within his Florida financial empire. Davis had set up his various enterprises so that they might continue in business without him. This proved impossible as the executors of his estate found he had $20 million in obligations and had left legacies of $2.6 million. They also had inheritance taxes to pay. The estate had less than $1 million in cash to meet over $33 million in obligations. This meant the executors had to start selling its assets.

Moreover, the estate's assets proved to be worth much less than the earlier estimates. When the executors filed Davis's will with the Dade County Court in 1964, the estate was

The hotel's large housekeeping staff poses for a portrait on the west side of the hotel near the Schultze and Weaver "covered walk," circa 1962. *Photo by Jim Leo, Boca Raton Historical Society.*

appraised at $86.6 million. Nixon Smiley, writing in the *Miami Herald* on December 12, 1965, traced the nose dive in Alcoa stock prices as among the many reasons for the great decline in Davis's wealth. When Davis retired as chairman, Alcoa sold for around $150 a share. When he died, that price had fallen to $50. Smiley also said that in his last years, Davis spent lavishly, "like a sailor on shore leave with his pockets bulging with money." His spending included the various companies, banks and land purchases he made for investments and also the luxuries he indulged in his personal life. He purchased Journey's End in 1949 and completely remodeled the large estate. When he discovered that noise from Old Cutler Road kept him from sleeping, he paid $235,000 to have it rerouted away from his house. He also owned an estate on Long Island, an apartment on Fifth Avenue, a house in the Bahamas and a fishing camp in the Keys. To move between these locations, and to more easily supervise his real estate holdings, he owned two airplanes and a helicopter. When the executors paid off the $20 million in debts, the $11 million in estate and inheritance taxes and the $2.6 million in legacies—such as the $1 million in cash, Journey's End and a yearly income to Evelyn Mitchell, Davis's secretary and companion in his last years—less than $54 million remained. Davis directed that this be divided into two trusts headquartered in Miami and Pittsburgh and used for charity,

A.V. Davis's acquisition of the resort signaled a new era for the hotel in many ways. For example, the multimillionaire often arrived via helicopter, shown here circa 1958. *Photo by Jim Leo, Boca Raton Historical Society.*

education, science and religious works. He also left inheritances to the heirs of his late brother, Edward K. Davis and to his stepdaughter, Dorothy Givens, the daughter of his second wife who had died in 1933. Smiley reported that, since the appraisal, the upturn in the economy had made the estate worth $60 million in 1965. In an ironic twist, in 1967 a Dade County judge approved fees of $6 million to the executors and law firms that handled Davis's estate.

In the summer of 1966, Davis's executors sold his Arvida stock to the Pennsylvania Railroad. The purchase of 3,274,000 shares at approximately $6 each, or about $19.6 million, gave the railroad control of the company. The "Pennsy" then sold 222,351 shares to Stockton, Whatley, Davin and Company "to assure continuity of experienced management." This left the railroad with about 51 percent of outstanding shares in the company. Stuart T. Saunders, chairman of the Pennsylvania Railroad, described the purchase as a major advance in the "Pennsy's" diversification program.

Beginning shortly after Whatley became president, Arvida built five high-rise condominiums during the 1960s, two on the south shore of Lake Boca Raton and three north of the inlet on the ocean. All apartment owners became members of the Boca

Raton Club, which, by the end of the decade, included a championship eighteen-hole golf course and a nine-hole "executive's course" at the hotel, and two additional eighteen-hole courses at a new Arvida development called Boca West. Members also had access to all the other hotel facilities and to the oceanfront Cabana Club. Although the twelve- to sixteen-story high-rises had their critics, Whatley defended their construction: "It seems to me you either stack them up and have plenty of land around you in the form of golf courses and open space, or you use every square inch of land, just carpet it with single houses in a continuous grid." Milton Weir also defended the condominiums, arguing that they satisfied the desire of many people to live by the sea.

Stuart Saunders took an active interest in the management of the Boca Raton Hotel and Club. Although L. Bert Stephens, a highly regarded hotel man, took over its direction, it still failed to be profitable. Both Saunders and Whatley believed that its limited season and lack of convention facilities kept the hotel from reaching its potential and competing with the newer hotels in Miami Beach and Fort Lauderdale.

In July 1967, Arvida secured a $25 million loan from the Aetna Life and Casualty Company to refinance and consolidate existing mortgages and to complete a $14 million expansion and modernization program at the hotel. Lacking air-conditioning, the hotel was unable to extend its season into the summer and fall months. As a partial answer to this problem, the hotel built the sixty-bedroom golf course villas near the nine-hole executive golf course. The air-conditioned villas allowed golfers to vacation in Boca Raton all year long.

This aerial view shows town houses, condos and golf courses of the Boca West development in the 1980s. *Boca Raton News Collection, Boca Raton Historical Society.*

One of Arvida's renovation projects was the creation of a convention center within the walls of the Schultze and Weaver–designed outdoor pool in the late 1960s. *Photo by Jim Leo, Boca Raton Historical Society.*

Plans for a new convention center, a twenty-six-story tower and the air-conditioning of the hotel followed. The convention center, called the Great Hall, incorporated the structure of the Schultze and Weaver–designed outdoor swimming pool with its four corner towers. With more than a half acre of space, the Great Hall contained ten meeting rooms with the latest audio-visual equipment, a large banquet/ballroom that could seat fifteen hundred, a huge all-electric, million-dollar kitchen and an exhibition area for products shown at conventions and meetings. It opened in the fall of 1968.

The new tower, called "300 feet of elegance" by the *Sun-Sentinel*, became for a brief period the tallest inhabited building between Jacksonville and Miami. Although some critics complained about its modern design and claimed that it clashed with the old hotel's architecture, an article in the *Palm Beach Daily News* dubbed it "Neo-Mizner" and said that it brought the "Mizner touch" once more into the spotlight. The New York firm of Warner, Burns, Toan and Lunde served as the principal architects, while Toro-Ferre of Puerto Rico, the designers of many Caribbean resorts, acted as consultants. William Cox, a native of Boca Raton and now a Coral Gables architect, supervised its construction. Plans called for the destruction of the southeastern wing of Mizner's inn with the new tower centered on his lakefront cloister.

The Davis era brought many dramatic changes to the hotel. In 1967, the southeastern corner of Mizner's Cloister Inn was demolished to make way for a new tower. *Boca Raton Historical Society.*

Johnson and Shapiro, in *Once Upon A Time*, say that Whatley changed the tower's original twenty-six floors to twenty-seven. With the tower's topping off, Whatley rode a construction elevator to the top and, stunned by the view, decided to add another floor for a restaurant. The ground floor of the new building served as a secondary lobby for the hotel, with a lounge and meeting rooms. On the second floor, overlooking Lake Boca Raton, the architects placed the Kingman Lounge, named for the artist of its mural. The third floor contained the mechanical and air-conditioning equipment, with two feet of concrete for sound control separating it from the fourth floor, where the guest rooms began. Each floor between the fourth and twenty-fourth contained twelve, twenty- by twenty-foot rooms. Stuart Saunders's close attention to details can be seen when Inez Croom, a New York interior designer who had completed his house and railroad car, received the contract for the tower's interiors. One source claimed the decor was "in keeping with the present Spanish theme."

Croom also designed the Presidential Suite on the twenty-fifth and twenty-sixth floors. Massive hand-carved Mediterranean-style doors with inlays of gold and turquoise gave entrance to the suite with its two-story living room, Indian silk Venetian draperies so heavy that their movement was powered by a one-horsepower motor, a dining room

The new tower is shown nearing completion at the southeast corner of the hotel in January 1969. *Boca Raton Historical Society.*

with a long, hand-carved table believed to have been part of Mizner's furnishings for the Cloister Inn, a library, a rarely used kitchen and four bedrooms and five baths. A guest could ascend to the duplex suite's second floor either by a marble staircase or private elevator. When the tower opened in November 1969, the suite cost $750 a night, and celebrities, such as Victor Borge, and presidents of top echelon companies occupied it "all the time" during its first year. The other halves of the these two floors contained "executive suites." On February 21, 1970, the restaurant at the top of the tower opened with a dinner for three hundred guests. The tower added 257 guest rooms and suites, giving the hotel a total of 657 rooms and the ability to stay open twelve months a year.

February 1970 also saw the opening of the second eighteen-hole golf course at Boca West, designed by Desmond Muirhead and Gene Sarazer, and the new modern, wood and glass, rambling million-dollar clubhouse, designed by William Cox and Charles Harrison Pawley of Coral Gables. A *Boca Raton News* article mentioned that Arvida planned two more golf courses for the 1,450-acre community of low-rise condominiums and single-family residences. Although the hotel remained known as a golfing destination, well-known professionals had served its tennis program since the 1930s. In 1972, the hotel played host to the inaugural Virginia Slims Tournament, which seventeen-year-old

This aerial view reveals the new profile of the Boca Raton Hotel and Club, circa 1970. At the center is the imposing 1969 tower, still Boca Raton's tallest building. *Boca Raton Historical Society*.

Guests enjoy the spectacular view of Lake Boca Raton and the ocean from the lounge atop the new tower at the Boca Raton Hotel, 1972. *Boca Raton Historical Society*.

Chris Evert won in a hard-fought match against Billie Jean King. Although she said that King was her most formidable opponent in over 160 tournaments, she still had to forego the first-place $25,000 award as she was still an amateur. She turned professional the following year.

In 1968, after years of negotiations and numerous government hearings, the Pennsylvania and New York Central railroads merged to create Penn Central, the nation's largest railroad. Stuart Saunders continued to serve as chairman of the combined companies. Less than four years later, the Penn Central declared bankruptcy. While Arvida remained unaffected by the problems of its parent company, in 1974 the American economy suffered a severe recession, with sales of Florida houses and condominiums brought to a halt. In 1972, Brown Whatley left the presidency and Arvida named thirty-seven-year-old Charles E. Cobb Jr., a California native and Stanford University business school graduate, as his successor. Cobb brought with him fellow California developers John Temple, who succeeded to the presidency when Cobb became chairman, and William Shubin, who headed Arvida's commercial and industrial development and created the company's Park of Commerce with its Broken Sound Golf Club. Again, Arvida suffered little from the recession as it had few debts and continued to receive modest profits. In the last years of the decade, when Florida's housing market began to recover, Arvida embarked on an aggressive development program and on plans to improve the Boca Raton Hotel and Club.

Since Addison Mizner proposed to build his one-thousand-room Castillo del Rey on the Boca Raton beach, an oceanfront hotel had been a dream of his successors. Now Arvida proposed to build a luxury hotel on its property at Sabal Point, directly across the lake from the hotel and club. Plans for the new hotel also included a new and modern cabana club to replace the aging and less convenient facility on South Ocean Boulevard. Although the Boca Raton City Council approved the hotel's permit in August 1976, some city residents opposed its construction, claiming the public would lose access to the beach. A petition drive forced an election that approved the council's action. Then a citizen's suit to block construction, claiming the public had acquired the right by custom to use the beach, failed in circuit court in June 1978, and Arvida immediately broke ground for the new hotel. Reflecting Charles Cobb's California background, Edward A. Killingsworth of Killingsworth, Brady and Associates from Long Branch received the commission to design the hotel. Killingsworth, a graduate of the University of Southern California, had designed the Kahala Hilton Hotel in Honolulu. Cobb selected Erickson Associates of Alhambra, California, as the interior designer and Dan Powell of Sausalito as the landscape architect.

The new hotel, named the Boca Beach Club, opened on December 19, 1980, to rave reviews from both local newspapers and travel writers from across the country. One called it a "smashing new nest of elegance"; another, the "sparkling diamond" in the "jewel-studded crown" of the Boca Raton Hotel and Club. Arvida, which had spent $20 million on its construction, also seemed pleased. L. Bert Stephens, the hotel's president, said that while the Boca Raton Hotel and Club had always been a symbol of elegance, it had needed an ocean setting: "Now we have a complete resort." Scott Morrison, the general manager of the complex, said that the older hotel had often become full of

This aerial view reveals the completed Beach Club in 1982. The Boca Inlet bridge is visible at the upper right. *Boca Raton Historical Society.*

convention people. The Boca Beach Club "was a social hotel…just what we needed." The Beach Club's manager, Swiss-born Alexander de Toth, said it brought "a lot of prestige to Boca Raton and the whole area."

The new hotel contained 212 rooms, with 147 oceanfront cabanas, ten loggias, five lounges and two restaurants. Guests traveled between the older hotel and the Beach Club by either pink bus or *Mizner's Dream*, a forty-four-foot yacht. The hotel had conducted a contest to name the yacht, with the winner receiving a complimentary weekend for two. The staff, in uniforms of gray, rose and tan, had a one-to-one ratio with guests. Arriving guests sat at a desk to register and staff offered champagne or chilled fruit juice. Room rates began at $200 a night and included breakfast, lunch and dinner. The Boca Beach Club's color scheme was "soft, luxurious and totally in keeping with the picturesque surroundings." One resident manager said, "The overall effect is similar in feeling to what Addison Mizner would be designing in the 1980s." The first party in the new Beach Club benefitted the Boca Raton Historical Society, with proceeds earmarked for the restoration of Boca Raton's historic town hall.

Although some city residents attempted to save it, bulldozers attacked and razed the old Cabana Club in January 1981. Preservationists did save one piece of the building. Its portico became a picnic shelter in Palm Beach County's beachfront park, just south of the inlet. Arvida replaced the Cabana Club with its most luxurious condominium complex. The Addison, designed by Paul Twitty of Schwab and Twitty of Palm Beach, consisted of two fifteen-story, long, thin towers designed in a sweeping curve and containing 178 apartments.

By the end of the 1970s, Mizner's dreams for Boca Raton were coming true. His oceanfront hotel had become a reality. After the Royal Palm Yacht and Country Club and University Park developments, Arvida had continued its western expansion with Boca West, Estancia, Paseos, Timbercreek, Millpond and Town Place. In cooperation with Federated Department stores, in 1979 it had developed Town Center shopping center, where soon branches of the nation's most elegant stores could be found. IBM, Germany's Siemens Corporation and other high-tech companies now called Boca Raton home, and Florida Atlantic University and the College of Boca Raton gave Mizner one college more than his dream. With the help of Arvida, Boca Raton had grown to become the destination of the cosmopolitan vacationer, the home of the sophisticated retiree and the workplace of trained professionals in many fields.

Chapter 5

The Boca Raton Resort & Club

By 1980, although the Penn Central had emerged from bankruptcy, it still felt the need for cash and decided to sell Arvida. While it failed to find a buyer for Arvida, in the spring of 1983 one appeared for the Boca Raton Hotel and Club. VMS Reality Partners, a group of three Chicago businessmen, agreed to pay $100 million for the hotel and sign a long-term contract for Arvida to continue managing it. Later in the year, when it seemed Penn Central might have a buyer for Arvida, Charles Cobb, who resigned as senior executive vice president and chief operating officer of Penn Central to rejoin his old company and his Arvida management team of almost twenty executives, backed by the billionaire Bass brothers of Texas, came up with the $196 million in cash needed to buy the company.

The partnership between Cobb, the executives and the Bass brothers only lasted a few months. By May, Walt Disney Productions had purchased Arvida for $200 million in its stock. Disney owned between fifteen thousand and twenty thousand acres of vacant land around Walt Disney World in central Florida and believed that Arvida's management could effectively develop the land. One source claimed Cobb saw the purchase as a chance to rise to the top of Disney's executive ladder, while all the Arvida executives believed they could realize an immediate financial windfall. The Bass brothers traded their 70 percent ownership of Arvida for a 7 percent stake in Disney. Raymond Watson, Disney's chairman, said, "Arvida gives us instant capability to develop our property in Florida." The acquisition also seemed to block a hostile takeover action directed at Disney. At the time of the merger, Charles Cobb claimed, "Our corporate culture is similar to Disney's—a commitment to quality, a commitment to the consumer, and a commitment to solving community problems."

Some on the Disney board and among its stockholders believed Watson's action in acquiring Arvida was entirely aimed at avoiding a hostile takeover. These disagreements over management led to Watson's ouster and the appointment of Michael Eisner as the new chairman. Eisner represented the entertainment side of the industry and failed to

This aerial view, looking east and south toward Boca Inlet, reveals the hotel and the Beach Club property north of the inlet, sometime in the late 1980s. *Boca Raton News Collection, Boca Raton Historical Society.*

appreciate Arvida's possible contribution. Arvida executives created an imaginative new proposal for a comprehensive mixed-use community near Orlando, though Disney's new management refused to accept the plans. During this period, Arvida remained actively involved in its Boca Raton developments. When it sold the Boca Raton Hotel and Club to VMS Realty Partners, it retained ownership of most land surrounding the hotel grounds. During the Disney years, it built Mizner Court, a five-story condominium on the lakefront at the north gate to the hotel grounds. The new condominium, designed by William Cox in "Neo-Mizner" style, contained apartments costing from $250,000 to $600,000 and offered owners membership in the Boca Raton Hotel and Club.

In 1987, Disney sold Arvida to JMB Reality Corporation of Chicago, ignoring the wishes of Charles Cobb and other executives who had proposed establishment of a limited partnership between Disney and Arvida management. When JMB agreed to pay $400 million for the company, Cobb said it came as "a total shock." One Arvida executive claimed the decision to sell culminated a relationship filled with "back-stabbing, vindictiveness and political battles." Most of the original Arvida executives had left the company before JMB took over the reins, and with their profits from the rise in Disney's stock price many established their own South Florida development companies.

In 1980, the Boca Raton Hotel and Club lost its long-held prestigious five-star rating from the *Mobil Travel Guide*. According to one source, the great emphasis on the details and service for the Boca Beach Club meant less concern for the "convention hotel."

Despite the many additions to the hotel, the beauty of the historic section is still evident in this 1985 photo of the courtyard. *Photo by Trumbull, Boca Raton News Collection, Boca Raton Historical Society.*

Another source condemned the ancient bathrooms in the Cloister Inn and Boca Raton Club buildings. No matter what the reason, Bert Stephens and his staff worked tirelessly to regain its fifth star, which happened in just two years. A decade later, the hotel decided to no longer allow ratings by either Mobil or the American Automobile Association. A spokesman said that the raters focused on crystal and marble, while the hotel used Mizner's wrought iron.

In 1985, Stephens retired, and Scott Morrison, who had been vice president of the company that operated the Kiawah Island Resort in South Carolina, became president. In a *Palm Beach Post* business profile, Morrison said mixing the business and social guests, as well as the club members, was his major problem. He claimed to solve it by keeping business and social guests separated and by making the club members feel special by giving them their own dining room. Morrison also said he appreciated the hotel's history and had staff members researching the original furnishings and Mizner's oriental rugs. If possible, he planned to replace some now-missing original furnishings with replicas. He also mentioned the recent $3 million renovation that had added the croquet court and refurbished 150 rooms and baths, and the continuing need to expand the meeting facilities.

By 1988, the hotel, which had never been extremely profitable, decided to change its image, although it was now Florida's only Mobil five-star and AAA five-diamond hotel. David Feder, the hotel's marketing director, pointed out in a *Boca Raton News* interview that between 1985 and 1986, 100,000 new hotel rooms were built in Florida, many in the Palm Beach, Fort Lauderdale and Miami area. "Five years ago, we didn't have any competition, now we have competition from all sides." Attempting to attract younger, more affluent guests, especially young double-income couples between ages thirty-five and forty-five, the hotel renovated more guest rooms, reconstructed its golf course and hired a tennis consulting service to market its twenty-two-court facility. In another appeal to the younger group, the hotel dropped its mandatory meal plan as many guests now ate off premises in Boca Raton restaurants and resented paying for the hotel meals. Michael Glennie, the hotel's new president, said, "Our main business is to fill hotel rooms... Before losing a single hotel room, we rather they stayed here and ate downtown." Glennie also recognized the hotel could improve its eight restaurants and said he planned to negotiate with top restaurateurs, who might run their own restaurants at the hotel. The hotel also purchased the Boca Golf and Tennis Club in October 1988. Located on Congress Avenue just north of Clint Moore Road, the club gave hotel guests access to additional recreational facilities, including a forty-thousand-square-foot clubhouse, another eighteen-hole golf course and seven more tennis courts. The clubhouse included racquetball courts and a fitness room.

The self-improvement "kick" and many makeovers resulted partially from the hotel hiring a New York City advertising agency and its launching of a $1 million marketing campaign. The old "image" campaign had run ads in upscale magazines like the *New Yorker* and *Architectural Digest*, with a hotel photograph and the single line, "Quite Simply the Best." The new campaign focused on the hotel's many amenities, showing "the hotel as a more lively, more fun, people place," according to Feder. The ad agency also suggested a name change. "We are truly more than a hotel, and should say so right up

The tower is the focus of this late 1980s photo featuring the "new" outdoor pool constructed in the late 1960s to replace the original saltwater pool. *Boca Raton News Collection, Boca Raton Historical Society.*

front." In line with its frugal management, after the old paper supplies ran out, in 1986 the hotel became the Boca Raton Resort & Club.

The hotel also dedicated its own championship golf course to "Slammin' Sam" Snead and the "Silver Scott" Tommy Armour, two of the three head golf professionals in the hotel's sixty-year history. Armour served from the opening of the Boca Raton Club in 1930 until 1955, with Snead succeeding him and serving until 1969. The ceremonies, part of the club's annual Pro-Am Golf Tournament in 1988, saw Snead and Armour's two grandsons among the players.

During the next year, VMS faced "cash-flow" problems. To combat these problems, it replaced its top management and laid off five hundred employees. By 1989, Xerox had joined the original three partners, and its representative to VMS took over as chairman and chief executive officer. A *New York Times* article on November 15, 1989, told of VMS's problems and mentioned that real estate–limited partnerships served as a principal form of tax shelter until the Tax Reform Act of 1986 eliminated most tax benefits. The *Times* said that most such partnerships had either sharply scaled back their operations, left the business or filed for bankruptcy. The new chairman said VMS had "liquid assets" to meet the company's obligations.

In September 1989, VMS announced plans to add a new, greatly enlarged convention center, a 279-room all-suite hotel, a golf clubhouse and a health spa, all designed to keep the resort competitive in the South Florida market. In February, the *Miami Herald* reported that VMS had representatives in Tokyo trying to find a buyer for the hotel. The *Herald* quoted Michael Glennie, who said the ambitious expansion plan made the sale necessary. The company recognized that raising $100 million for the project required "finding a joint-venture partner or we need to sell the property and retain long-term management…We're now focusing our efforts on the second option."

The company found no buyers in Japan, although in 1993, Boca Raton Hotel and Club Limited Partnership bought the resort, and Boca Raton Management Company replaced VMS in directing its activities. John Temple was a principal of the management company. The new management refinanced $150 million in debt and began the planned expansion of the resort's facilities, having construction well in hand when H. Wayne Huizenga's Florida Panthers Holding, Inc. bought the resort for $325 million in March 1997. At the same time, the Panthers company purchased the Hyatt Regency Pier 66 and Radisson Bahia Mar resorts for $225 million and the Registry Resort and Club in Naples for $99.5 million. The year before, Huizenga, billionaire owner of the Florida Panthers, a National Hockey League team, had created the holding company and raised $66 million in a public stock offering. The acquisition of the resorts resulted in the issuance of approximately 4.9 million more shares of Florida Panther Holdings common stock. The investors in Boca Raton Hotel and Club Limited Partnership and the Boca Raton Management Company greatly profited from the stock deal.

John Temple of the management company and former Arvida president countered criticism that the resort had left local hands, saying that only he of the principals of the old company actually lived in Florida. A representative of Panthers Holding pointed out that Fort Lauderdale was only "seventeen miles down the road" and that local people held the Florida Panthers stock. City council member and later mayor Steven Abrams said that, once he knew that Huizenga had no plans to build a stadium in the middle of a golf course, "I thought [the sale] was a good thing." In fact, he said that since Florida Panthers Holding was a public company, local people had greater opportunities to participate in the hotel's ownership than they had before under the limited partnership.

H. Wayne Huizenga, Florida Panthers' chairman, had lived in Fort Lauderdale since his family moved there from Chicago in 1952, when he was fifteen. A graduate of Pine Crest School, he attended Calvin College in Grand Rapids, Michigan, and joined the Army Reserves in 1959. By the time he purchased the Boca Raton Resort & Club, he had founded and grown Waste Management, Inc. into the largest waste disposal company in the country. He had the same success with Blockbuster Video, taking the small company public in 1989 and then launching rapid growth. From nineteen stores, it grew into a global enterprise with thousands of locations in eleven countries. In 1994, he sold the company to Viacom for $8.4 billion in stock, just before the market in video rentals collapsed. In 1996, he created AutoNation, which became America's largest automotive dealer with 370 locations.

In South Florida, Huizenga's reputation stemmed from his ownership of three major league sports teams. Beginning with 50 percent ownership of the Miami Dolphins in 1990, he bought out the other shares and became full owner in 1993. He became the initial owner of the Florida Marlins baseball team, which he saw win a World Series before selling it to Boca Raton's John Henry in 1998. He also introduced hockey into the area with his Florida Panthers, which he sold in 2001. Huizenga's business philosophy has always seemed uncomplicated: buy low, take a company public and then sell high.

Huizenga also tried to quiet fears of his motives for buying the Boca Raton Resort & Club by saying, "This is a very exciting day for our company; with this transaction we have added a very profitable asset and a talented management team." He also said he planned to keep Michael Glennie as president. Glennie added, "Absolutely nothing will change. Mr. Huizenga loves the quality of the place and wants us to continue plans to upgrade the facility."

In 1998, Huizenga continued to add to his hotel empire by buying the Arizona Biltmore in Phoenix for $290 million and the Edgewater Beach Hotel in Naples for $41.2 million. In 1999, he changed the company name to Boca Resorts, Inc., and announced that while growth was very important, profitability was equally, if not more, important. In July 2001, he sold the Florida Panthers to a group of fans for $101 million, ridding the company of its biggest drain on profits. In December of the same year, he sold off the Arizona Biltmore for $335 million, liquidating a misfit property, the only company hotel located outside of Florida, while earning around $40 million in profits in three years on the sale.

Many of the improvements set in motion at the Boca Raton Resort & Club before Huizenga's purchase were completed in this period. The $10 million Tennis and Fitness Center opened in 1997. According to the resort, the new facility included a two-story, Mizner-style clubhouse with a viewing deck and a pro shop with eighteen clay courts that utilized the latest technology, allowing the courts to maintain a consistent level of surface moisture. The fitness center included state-of-the-art equipment, with personal trainers and classes in yoga, pilates and aerobics. The Mizner Center opened in January 1998.

The new 128,000-square-foot convention center contained numerous meeting rooms, over 80,000 square feet of function space and an area for meetings of up to eighteen hundred people. Its 9,000-square-foot kitchen could prepare more than four thousand meals a day, and eighteen-wheeled trucks could be driven into its ballrooms. A *Boca Raton News* article of early 1998 said the center's style was an extension of the resort's original design by Addison Mizner. On both the exterior and interior, the architects used the Romanesque arch of Mizner's entrance to the Cloister Inn. They also used the lacy filigree pattern that served as the pediment on the entrance pavilion of the inn on the center's western façade. A huge cast-stone and tile fireplace graced the massive interior assembly space. Venetian coats of arms, Florentine-style villa paintings, colorful carpets and a number of antique banners from Geist's club decorated the center. Michael Glennie called the Mizner Center "probably the single most important project that we've done." He said there had been an imbalance between meeting and hotel rooms.

During the summer months, the hotel had to have convention business to remain open as there was never enough leisure demand. All too often, the hotel filled its meeting space, although many guest rooms stayed vacant. The summer convention business allowed by the Mizner Center also meant that hotel employees had twelve-month jobs. Glennie said that before the center the hotel laid off one thousand people in April only to try to rehire them in December. "You can imagine the logistical training nightmare that was." One of the new center's first events, a two-day enterprise conference sponsored by Microsoft's Bill Gates, brought 650 Latin American business and government leaders to the resort. Gates must have been impressed. He raised his stake in Boca Resorts, Inc. to two million shares, or about 5 percent of the total.

The resort's new 128,000-square-foot convention center, known as the Mizner Center, opened in January of 1998. *Photo by Thomas Hart Shelby, courtesy LXR Luxury Resorts.*

When Arvida sold the Boca Raton Hotel and Club to VMS, it retained ownership of the undeveloped land around its boundaries. Realizing the profitability of development rights, Boca Resorts carved out a 7.4-acre plot from the golf course driving range for a fifteen-lot subdivision. Mizner Lake Estates, a collection of custom-built luxury houses ranging from five thousand to fourteen thousand square feet, sold for $2.5 million and higher. The residents of Mizner Lake became members of the club and could also receive complete hotel guest services such as room service and housekeeping.

On February 6, 2001, the resort celebrated its seventy-fifth birthday. More than two thousand members and guests, clad in various shades of pink, filled the courtyard to hear Glennie, Huizenga, Boca Raton Mayor Carol Hanson and Palm Beach County Commissioner Mary McCarty; to drink forty-five cases of pink champagne, twenty cases of white zinfandel and ten of Tequilla Rose Liqueur; and to eat Boca pink M&Ms and a twenty-foot-high pink birthday cake. Since the resort wished to share the celebration with the world, it also sponsored a live Internet webcast.

In time for the birthday party, the resort had completed a new extension of the main lobby that now opened to the cloister overlooking the lake designed by Marion Sims Wyeth in 1931. The new open space, formerly the Patio Royale, contained a casual bar, a large new fountain and elaborately decorated ceiling panels. It also provided an improved entrance to the Cathedral Dining Room and to Lucca, a new Italian restaurant run by Drew Nieporent of New York's Nobu and Tribeca Grill. Bar Luna filled the west end of Mizner's lounge and used his cast-stone window frames and his fireplace in its decor. On the eve of the celebration, former President Bill Clinton spoke to employees and clients of Morgan Stanley Dean Witter during their annual company conference at the resort. Clinton, in his first talk since leaving the presidency, received $100,000 for his effort.

In December 2001, the resort opened both the new golf clubhouse and its Spa Palazzo. The thirty-six-thousand-square-foot golf clubhouse was a $9 million investment that included luxurious locker rooms with butler service, a pro shop and a casual restaurant and bar with a view of the course's eighteenth hole. Located directly west of the hotel and its trellised walkway, the Mediterranean-style building contained a large deck overlooking the golf course, which received a $10 million reconstruction. The $17 million Spa Palazzo, modeled on the Alhambra Palace, according to the resort, "is designed to replicate paradise on earth." Its fifty thousand square feet housed forty-four treatment suites, a wet room, sunning terraces and palatial gardens featuring waterfalls, whirlpools and a spa pool. A large two-story lounge, with three immense windows with cast-stone Gothic surrounds, overlooked the pool and served as the waiting room.

Just three months later, in February 2002, the resort opened the Yacht Club, its eight-story, 112 guest rooms and luxury suites hotel addition designed to resemble a Venetian palace. All rooms had a view of the marina and Lake Boca Raton, and those above the fourth floor could also see the ocean. The facility offered butler service, a concierge lounge, meeting rooms and thirty-two new yacht slips. Michael Glennie said that in only a few years, a large yacht had grown from 75 to 150 feet. The new marina could accommodate boats even larger than 150 feet. The Yacht Club had some of the hotel's most expensive rooms. Glennie explained that over the last four or five years, "the most expensive ones sell out first." A reporter for the *Wall Street Journal* visited the resort on

Located directly west of the hotel, overlooking the eighteenth hole, the golf clubhouse opened in December 2001. *Photo by Thomas Hart Shelby, courtesy LXR Luxury Resorts.*

The beautiful Spa Palazzo, modeled on the Alhambra Palace, features a large two-story lounge with three immense windows overlooking a pool. *Photo by Michael Caldwell, courtesy LXR Luxury Resorts.*

In 2002, the resort opened the Yacht Club, an eight-story luxury suites addition designed to resemble a Venetian palace. *Photo by Thomas Hart Shelby, courtesy LXR Luxury Resorts.*

her "long quest for the perfect spa experience." Calling the high-rise tower a "tacky pink" and the Boca Beach Club "institutional," she claimed "the Yacht Club [was] by far the best place to stay now at the hotel." She said the guest room decor was elegant and comfortable. While she completely enjoyed her spa experience, one of her stories harkened back to the fabled days of Mizner and Geist. She claimed she had to walk from the spa to her Yacht Club room in her robe, past "Tag-and-Label conventioneers" at the Monkey Bar.

David Feder returned as president in 2001, when Michael Glennie left to head up a company acquiring hotels in Japan. Feder, who had served as managing director of the Arizona Biltmore, came back to Boca Raton to oversee the completion of the Yacht Club and Spa. He also guided Boca Resort, Inc.'s action in receiving permission from the city council to build an eight-story, 163-room lodge with a restaurant, a twelve-thousand-square-foot convention center, a 776-car parking deck, fitness club, pool, cabanas and spa on Sabal Point, and an eight-story, 55- unit condominium across AIA from the Boca Beach Club. After the council approved the projects, residents of Presidential Place, a neighboring oceanfront condominium and former mayor Emil Danciu sued the city, seeking a court-ordered referendum to allow residents to vote on the resort's expansion. Mayor Steven Abrams said he understood how people living close to the hotel might be upset. On the other hand, Mayor Abrams said the hotel continued as both a landmark and the city's largest taxpayer, and "it's within the hotel's property rights to renovate and expand."

In a July 2003 interview in the *Palm Beach Post*, Feder emphasized the hotel's good economic shape. While the revenues of most hotels fell after the attack on the World Trade Center, he said the Boca Raton Resort & Club had very good years. It also completed its many additions and had refurbished guest rooms and suites in the cloister, tower and Beach Club to "the level of luxury and comfort for which the resort was known." Feder said the Boca Resort, Inc. stock, which currently traded at thirteen dollars, should be priced at eighteen to twenty dollars. One reason for its low price stemmed from Huizenga's ownership of only 17.4 percent of common stock, though he controlled 98.5 percent of the voting shares. The company had been structured this way to comply with National Hockey League rules. According to an analyst who closely followed Boca Resorts, Inc., after Huizenga sold the team, he should have changed the company's voting structure. This failure resulted in its undervaluation, and many rumors of takeover talks swirled around the company. Feder denied that the company was for sale.

Then, just over a year later, on October 20, 2004, the Boca Resort, Inc. announced that it had been purchased by the private equity firm the Blackstone Group for $1.25 billion. What had changed? In a year's time, the stock price had risen to $18.76 and Blackstone had agreed to a 28 percent premium, offering $24.00 dollars a share. Blackstone also agreed to assume the company's $160 million in debt. Huizenga said he had an obligation to make money for his stockholders. "We've been in it now for more than seven years, so its time to make money for your shareholders." One observer pointed out that Huizenga Holdings, Inc., his family holding company, owned about 50 percent in Boca Resort, Inc. and stood to make as much as $500 million on the sale, while Huizenga's personal 17 percent ownership could bring around $197 million. Blackstone's acquisition of Boca Resorts, Inc. at first seemed "out of the blue." Then it was realized that Blackstone had purchased Huizenga's down-scale Extended Stay America hotel chain earlier in the year.

Stephen Schwarzman, a principal in Blackstone and a part-time Palm Beach resident (he owned Four Winds, a 1937 ocean-to-lake residence designed by Maurice Fatio for Edward F. Hutton), said, "Our long history and expertise in managing prestige hotels around the world will be invaluable in working with management to enhance the value for everyone involved in this quality group of hotels and resorts." A Blackstone spokesman mentioned the company had been involved "at the top end" of the hotel industry, having owned the Savoy Group, which included the Savoy, Claridge's, the Connaught and the Berkeley in London.

Schwarzman became another of the Boca Raton Resort & Club's "bigger-than-life" owners. A Yale graduate with a Harvard MBA, he joined Lehman Brothers in 1972 and became a partner six years later. Peter G. Peterson, chairman of the company and a former Nixon secretary of commerce, became his mentor, and after an internal shake up at Lehman Brothers, the two founded the Blackstone Group in 1985. Schwarzman created the name from *schwarz*, or "black" in German, and *petros*, or "stone" in Greek. Peterson was of Greek ancestry. According to James B. Stewart in his *New Yorker* article on Schwarzman, it quickly became the leader in managing "so-called alternative assets such as private-equity, real-estate, and hedge funds." By the time Blackstone bought Boca Resorts, Inc., it was the world's largest manager of alternative assets, with $88 billion, and had control of 112 companies, with a combined value of nearly $200 billion.

The historic low-profile hotel is nestled between the Great Hall and tower at the left, and the newer Yacht Club and Mizner Center at the right in this 2005 photo. *Photo courtesy Peter Lorber.*

Private equity, the sanitized name for leveraged buyouts, generates capital gains instead of income with taxes at only 15 percent.

Like the Boca Raton Resort & Club's earlier owners, Schwarzman also lived well. He paid $37 million for John D. Rockefeller Jr.'s former thirty-five-room apartment in Park Avenue's most prestigious building; $20.5 million for Four Winds, which he enlarged and completely rebuilt; $34 million for a house and eight acres in the Hamptons; and owned an estate in Saint-Tropez and a beachfront property in Jamaica. He had also been active in public life, serving on the boards of the New York Public Library, the Frick Collection and the New York City Ballet, and as chairman of Washington's Kennedy Center. Schwarzman received major press exposure as a result of his multimillion-dollar sixtieth birthday party held at the Park Avenue armory on February 14, 2007. The publicity continued during the months when he took Blackstone Group public. The prospectus revealed that Schwarzman would take out $677.2 million and would keep a 24 percent ownership stake in the company valued at around $8 billion. During 2007, Blackstone also bought Equity Office Properties, a company owning large office buildings in many cities, for $39 billion, and Hilton Hotels for over $20 billion.

Blackstone took control of Boca Resorts during the first week of December 2004. The new owners immediately fired David Feder, replacing him as president with French-born Jean-Jacques Pergant, formerly with the Savoy Group in London. Pergant said he planned no major changes as the staff impressed him with its willingness to do the right thing, "with a great degree of service orientation." He said he planned to refurbish the hotel lobby, restaurants and golf villas, and renovate the Boca Beach Club. Feder stayed in Palm Beach County, becoming the president of PGA National Resorts and Club in Palm Beach Gardens. In 2006, he moved to Miami Beach, where he served as president and general manager of the Fontainebleau Resort.

Early in 2005, Blackstone changed the name of Boca Resorts, Inc. to LXR Luxury Resorts and announced the addition of five resorts in the Caribbean, three in Florida, six in the Western United States, two in New York and one in London to make a network of twenty-one properties. Blackstone acquired most of these properties when it bought Wyndham International. The new Florida hotels included the Reach and Casa Marina in Key West and Buena Vista Palace at Walt Disney World. Blackstone said it planned to spend $400 million to improve the resorts, turning them into "true luxury showpieces." LXR also named architect/decorator Thierry Despont to redo the lobby area of the 1930 Schultze and Weaver Boca Raton clubhouse. French born and École des Beaux-Arts trained, Despont decorated the lobby of Claridge's in London for Blackstone and served American clients such as Bill Gates, Ralph Lauren, Leslie Wexner and Calvin Klein. Despont claimed he based his design for the Schultze and Weaver lobby on historical research and that its appearance would revert to a Mizner aesthetic. The new decor included a light beige and white ceiling, slate and stone floors, new carpets to echo the floors and vaguely art deco white leather furniture. In opening the north wall of the main two-story-high section of the lobby and placing service desks and waiting areas into alcove spaces, he greatly improved traffic flow in what was often a very crowded part of the hotel. The opened section at the east end of the lobby created by Huizenga's renovations rarely saw use. The low ceiling made the water fountain seem extremely loud and a quiet conversation was almost impossible. Despont's solution opened the space, with high, modern, metal, Gothic-style columns and arches supporting a glass ceiling, similar to Santiago Calatrava's Oriente Station in Lisbon, Portugal. He also removed the fountain. Despont's only change in Mizner's Cloister Inn came with the enclosing of the loggia with high French doors inside the original columns.

Designer Alexandra Champalimaud completely renovated the former Golf Villas, now called the Boca Bungalows. The 130-room hotel "emulates the glamour and sophistication of 1920s Hollywood hide-aways" in their secluded setting north of the resort. According to a resort news release, Champalimaud balanced dark woods, white linen furnishings and artwork to create their dramatic design. The resort also opened new restaurants: Old Homestead Steak House with 280 seats on the second floor of the golf clubhouse and Cielo on the top of the tower. Cielo featured modern Tuscan cuisine in "a striking contemporary decor" created by New York architects Bentel and Bentel who designed the Modern, the new restaurant for the Museum of Modern Art. Thierry Despont said that all of the changes wrought by LXR had helped the resort to "return to casual life in an elegant environment." Certainly the Mizner concept that most of his successors followed of creating a hotel where comfort and luxury predominated remained a goal of the new owners.

Arvida's Golf Villas, located just north of the resort, were remodeled as the Boca Bungalows in 2005. *Photo by Thomas Hart Shelby, courtesy LXR Luxury Resorts.*

Atop the "Great Hall," a glimpse of the hotel's history is still visible. The north façade of the former hotel pool can be seen in this photo—now just another sunny deck. *Photo by Thomas Hart Shelby, courtesy LXR Luxury Resorts.*

Six months after taking ownership of the hotel, Blackstone Group also purchased the T-Rex office park in Boca Raton for $193 million. The park, originally the home of IBM, where it created the first personal computer, had several owners since IBM sold it for $46 million in 1996. Numerous sales—including those to the school board for Don Estridge Middle School, the city for a new library, the large de Hoernle park and Mizner Bark dog park, the regional transit authority for a new Tri-rail station and several private sales for housing and shopping developments—reduced the original 550 acres of land to around 123 when purchased by Blackstone. The IBM complex, originally designed by architects Marcel Breuer and Robert F. Gatje, was renamed Boca Corporate Center and Campus. A revamping included hurricane-resistant glass, renovated lobbies and, in general, the creation of a more luxurious setting for the rental offices. Shortly after its purchase, LXR Luxury Resorts donated $250,000 for the development of the city's de Hoernle Park.

Among other changes at the Boca Raton Resort & Club, LXR agreed to scale down Huizenga's plans for Sabal Point, ending up with one new condominium on the point with no construction of the west side of AIA. Since everyone seemed to believe the Boca Beach Club was stuck in 1980 and needed to be moved to the twenty-first century, the resort hired Andree Putman, the "glam eminence" who placed her stamp on Morgans in New York, to overhaul the "aging" hotel. She planned to add forty new rooms, a new restaurant and forty-six cabanas. Calling her styling the "futuro-green look," she planned to install plank floors, blond furnishings and white leather. In 2000, the city council gave Huizenga permission to add ninety-six hotel rooms, either over or on the resort's Great Hall site. When the Blackstone Group proposed to change these plans, asking for a building of sixty-two condominiums on the west side of the entry drive, opposition arose from residents of Royal Palm Yacht and Country Club on issues of massiveness and traffic congestion. Russ Flicker, president for development and Anne Hersley-Hankins, director of corporate communications, claimed development on the west side would be better for Royal Palm, as less of the building would actually touch Camino Real, and pointed out that the original proposal would have blocked lake views. They also mentioned that the resort wanted to do what was best for the community. Flicker said, "We live here," while Hersley-Hankins emphasized, "We're going to be here a long time. It doesn't make sense to have unhappy neighbors." While it's always impossible to please every neighbor, LXR Luxury Resorts certainly brought a fresh look to Mizner's legendary inn.

Bibliography

My collection of materials for this history began in the 1970s, when, for a number of years, I was a member of the Boca Raton Hotel and Club. During this time, I gained a great appreciation for the wonderful architecture and the overall ambiance of the Mizner and Schultze and Weaver buildings and even the old Cabana Club. This collection included newspaper clippings, magazine articles and other materials, such as hotel publicity releases. My research became more focused when I began work on my Mizner book and the histories of Palm Beach County and Boca Raton. I have read the *Palm Beach Post* and *Times* from around 1915 to the 1950s at the Historical Society of Palm Beach County and the *Palm Beach Daily News* for around the same period in the archives of the *Post*. The same is true of the *Boca Raton News* at the Boca Raton Historical Society, the *Delray Beach News* at the Delray Beach Public Library and the *Miami Herald* at its archives. I have also consulted vertical files on Mizner, Schultze and Weaver, Marion Sims Wyeth, Maurice Fatio and the various owners of the hotel at the Historical Society of Palm Beach County, the Miami-Dade Public Library and the Boca Raton Historical Society. These have included interviews with, and oral histories of, some of the individuals mentioned in the text. The Internet has been very helpful for researching specific topics in the *New York Times*.

Books

Ayers, R. Wayne. *Florida's Grand Hotels from the Gilded Age.* Charleston, SC: Arcadia Publishing, 2005.

Carr, Charles C. *Alcoa: An American Enterprise.* New York: Rinehart and Co., 1952.

Curl, Donald W. *Mizner's Florida: American Resort Architecture.* New York: The Architectural History Foundation, 1984.

————. *Palm Beach County: An Illustrated History.* Northridge, CA: Windsor Publications, 1986.

Curl, Donald W., and John F. Johnson. *Boca Raton: A Pictorial History.* Virginia Beach, VA: The Donning Co., 1990.

DeGeorge, Gail. *The Making of a Blockbuster: How Wayne Huizenga Built a Sports and Entertainment Empire from Trash, Grit, and Video Tape.* New York: John Wiley and Son, 1990.

Ettorre, Tony. *Arvida: A Business Odyssey.* Coral Springs, FL: An ECI Publication, 1991.

Florida Architecture of Addison Mizner. With a new introduction by Donald W. Curl. New York: Dover Publications, 1992. Originally published by William Helburn, Inc., 1928.

Gillis, Susan, and the Boca Raton Historical Society. *Boomtime Boca: Boca Raton in the 1920s.* Charleston, SC: Arcadia Publishing Co., 2007.

Johnson, Stanley, and Phyllis Shapiro. *Once Upon a Time: The Story of Boca Raton.* Miami: The Arvida Corp., 1987.

Lamonaca, Marianne, and Jonathan Mogul, eds. *Grand Hotels of the Jazz Age: The Architecture of Schultze and Weaver.* New York: Princeton Architectural Press, 2005.

Ling, Sally J. *Small Town, Big Secrets: Inside the Boca Raton Army Air Field During World War II.* Charleston, SC: The History Press, 2005.

Nolan, David. *Fifty Feet in Paradise: The Booming of Florida.* New York: Harcourt Brace Jovanovich, 1984.

Pratt, Theodore. *The Story of Boca Raton.* St. Petersburg, FL: Great Outdoors Publishing Co., 1969.

Vickers, Raymond B. *Panic In Paradise: Florida's Banking Crash of 1926.* Tuscaloosa and London: The University of Alabama Press, 1994.

Articles

Curl, Donald W. "Addison Mizner and the Palm Beach Style." *Florida Forum* (Summer 1987).

————. "Boca Raton and the Florida Land Boom of the 1920s." *Tequesta* (April 1993).

Edgerton, Giles. "Great Modern Hotels: The Ritz-Carlton Cloister of Boca Raton." *Arts and Decoration* (April 1926).

Fryzel, Louis. "The Dream of Addison Mizner." *Fiesta* (May 1970).

Lincoln, Freeman. "The Man Who is Buying Up Florida." *Fortune Magazine* (September 1987).

McCormick, Bernard. "Boca Raton: Tradition vs. the Times." *Gold Coast Pictorial* (Summer 1971).

Smiley, Nixon. "He Often Spent Not Wisely, But Too Well." *Miami Herald*, December 12, 1965.

————. "The Myth That Outgrew the Man." *Miami Herald*, December 12, 1965.